Workshopping the Canon for Democracy and Justice

Mary E. Styslinger
University of South Carolina

NCTE
National Council of Teachers of English
340 N. Neil St., Suite #104, Champaign, Illinois 61820
www.ncte.org

Manuscript Editor: Bonny Graham

Staff Editor: Cynthia Gomez

Interior Design: Jenny Jensen Greenleaf

Cover Design: Pat Mayer

Portions of this text and student work were previously published in NCTE journals, including *English Journal, Talking Points,* and *Voices from the Middle*. Used with permission.

ISBN 978-0-8141-0096-7 (print); ISBN 978-0-8141-0097-4 (ebook);
ISBN 978-0-8141-0098-1 (PDF)

It is the policy of NCTE in its journals and other publications to provide a forum for the open discussion of ideas concerning the content and the teaching of English and the language arts. Publicity accorded to any particular point of view does not imply endorsement by the Executive Committee, the Board of Directors, or the membership at large, except in announcements of policy, where such endorsement is clearly specified.

NCTE provides equal employment opportunity (EEO) to all staff members and applicants for employment without regard to race, color, religion, sex, national origin, age, physical, mental or perceived handicap/disability, sexual orientation including gender identity or expression, ancestry, genetic information, marital status, military status, unfavorable discharge from military service, pregnancy, citizenship status, personal appearance, matriculation or political affiliation, or any other protected status under applicable federal, state, and local laws.

Every effort has been made to provide current URLs and email addresses, but because of the rapidly changing nature of the Web, some sites and addresses may no longer be accessible.

Library of Congress Control Number: 2023935126

For my students and colleagues–
past, present, and future.
You are my teachers.
You inspire me to think and try harder.

Contents

Acknowledgments

This book could not have been written without the inspiration and guidance I have gained from students I have been privileged to teach and learn from. Big Sean once said, "It's evolution, man. Eventually the student becomes the teacher." My students and colleagues are my teachers. I am grateful to all of you. Know that you have made a difference in what I think, believe, and do. Because of you, I am a better teacher and learner for democracy and justice as evidenced in the theories I now hold, the curriculum I now teach, and the pedagogy I now practice.

I would especially like to acknowledge and thank the students and teachers who have shared their ideas in the pages of this book: Sarah Bortscheller, Ryan Browne, Sara Cain, Kelsey Covell, Isis Davis, Carson Duthu, Rollins Fish, Anna Maria Gardiner, Kathryn Schmalz Gibb, Reagan Glover, Michael Gore, Hannah Gresham, Caroline Hardin, Kayla Hyatt Hostetler, Helen Long, Franny Masella, Bridges Michel, Margaret Mitchell, Jillian Obregon, Ashley Pendley, Lori Rutledge, Jenna Safran, Elizabeth Schell, Stephanie Sharpe, Nicole Walker, Joshua Whisnant, Courtney Wolfe, and Dallas Zuniga. Thank you for lending your voices and sharing your models. Schools are better places because of you.

And last, I would like to thank the editorial team at the National Council of Teachers of English for believing this book into being, especially Bonny Graham and Kurt Austin. None of this would have been possible without your professional commitment and expertise.

Introduction: Rewriting for Change

This is what love does: It makes you want to rewrite the world. It makes you want to choose the characters, build the scenery, guide the plot.

—David Levithan, *Every Day*

Workshopping the Canon, this book's predecessor, was written to bridge the divide between the teaching of literature and the teaching of literacy. When we workshop the canon, we actively and purposefully partner classical texts with a variety of high-interest genres within a reading and writing workshop structure, aligning the teaching of literature with what we have come to recognize as best practices in the teaching of literacy. Through workshopping, we are able to bridge literary, theoretical, and pedagogical divides. Since writing this book, however, I have realized that this is not enough.

We live in tumultuous times. As this book is being written, two pandemics pervade US communities: COVID-19 and racism. While we now have a coronavirus vaccine, there is no immunization against discrimination. The deaths of Tanisha Anderson, Ahmaud Arbery, Michael Brown, Philando Castile, Stephon Clark, Michelle Cusseaux, George Floyd, Eric Garner, Freddie Gray, Botham Jean, Atatianna Jefferson, Trayvon Martin, Tamir Rice, Aura Rosser, Walter Scott, Alton Sterling, Breonna Taylor, Daunte Wright, and so many others have sparked an ongoing series of protests against systemic racism and police brutality. While most demonstrations have been peaceful, some have led to riots, vandalism, looting, and arson. In response, police officers and federal agents have used batons, tear gas, pepper spray, and rubber bullets on protestors, bystanders, and journalists.

Our streets and Capitol bear evidence of political and civic unrest. More than twenty years ago, Glasgow (2001) wrote about the polarization of American society in *English Journal*, and her words seem even more pressing today: "In an increasingly abrasive and polarized American society, social justice education has the potential to prepare citizens who are sophisticated in their understanding of diversity and group interaction, able to critically evaluate social institutions, and committed to working democratically with diverse others" (p. 54). In the past few years, I have thought about these words and pondered how we could utilize workshopping structures and strategies to teach for democracy and justice and bridge divides greater than those between literature and literacy.

Too often, social justice is an espoused ideal with little practical application. It's a theory discussed in college classrooms, the metaphorical ivory tower. But there is a need for middle and secondary curriculum that expands our understandings and perspectives of justice, equity, diversity, inclusion, and pedagogy that both reflects and fosters dispositions and skills expected for democracy. "Right thinking requires right doing," Freire (2001, p. 1) advised. We need examples of social justice teaching in the context of the language arts classroom, especially with a curriculum already familiar to middle and secondary teachers.

Workshopping the Canon for Democracy and Justice is a book rewritten during uncertain times to show teachers how to create and conduct a workshop focused on social justice issues relevant and critical to middle and secondary learners and citizens. Through workshopping, teachers can foster democratic dispositions and skills as they explore justice-oriented units. However, unlike its predecessor, *Workshopping the Canon*, this book offers readers a choice of focusing units on core canonical texts, demonstrating how to workshop these literary works for social justice, or working to disrupt and displace the canon, often viewed as a literary representation of power, by teaching a topically and thematically related young adult text. Another notable difference, each chapter begins with a quotation from a contemporary text rather than passages from classical literature. More critical essential questions interweave texts and bind units. Other genres, including young adult novels, short stories, informational texts, picture books, music, art, movies, and social media, are again included in the appendixes, but the inclusion of more diverse resources that make current societal and global connections, foster multiple perspectives, prompt critical thinking, and include primary voices is accentuated.

Workshopping the Canon for Democracy and Justice is a practical text. This book both adopts and adapts foundational reading and writing workshop structures for democratic and justice teaching in the context of the middle and secondary classroom and curriculum. Along with providing detailed suggestions for implementing workshop structures and strategies that foster democratic skills and dispositions, this book includes teacher examples and classroom artifacts. Whereas much has already been written about reading and writing workshops, democratic principles and practices, and social justice education, it is important to interweave and envision these ideas for middle and high school classrooms in the context of a familiar curriculum.

In reimagining this book, I draw on my experiences as a classroom teacher, as a teaching team member for a statewide reading initiative, as a director of a National Writing Project site, as an educator of new teachers at a state university, and as a colleague of so many inspirational teachers who surround me at the university, secondary, middle, and elementary levels. I dedicate this book to the students and colleagues I have been privileged to learn with over the past thirty years. They have pushed me to think and try harder. They have prompted and guided my critical awareness of injustice and inequities. They have helped me realize that our classroom curriculum and pedagogy can be a catalyst for positive change in the world.

I would be remiss if I didn't acknowledge my own positions in writing this book. I resemble the majority of the current English teacher population in the United States: white, female, cisgender, middle class, middle-aged, able-bodied, and heterosexual (Boser, 2014). My first language is English. I am unequivocally and irrefutably privileged. I have a job at a university, a house in the suburbs, two children, a cat, and a dog. I am one of the "nice, white teachers" Sinclair (2018) writes about who had trouble listening to colleagues of color when they described my complicity when I failed to confront systems of oppression. For too many years, I did not question my whiteness, white supremacy, or white emotions of guilt and shame (Love, 2020). I believed I was doing the right thing by teaching *To Kill a Mockingbird*. I thought it was better not to see race in my classroom and to search for commonalities rather than to celebrate differences among students. Was my "neutrality" a mask for racism (Kendi, 2019)? Like many of the teachers who will read this book, I have come to social justice teaching late. Unlike my smarter students and colleagues, I have had to catch up on reading over the past decades. But like a lot of teachers today, I am waking up. I won't say that I know better, because I am only coming to know. But I have tried to listen more, talk less, think harder, and do better.

This book is a work in progress. Curricula and teaching for democracy and justice will never be finished. And there will be some who say this book does not go far enough. That it is too safe. Too moderate. They are right. But this text, filled with teacher voices, useful models, and helpful ideas, is written to foster initial agency for change. My hope in writing *Workshopping the Canon for Democracy and Justice* is to provide middle and high school English teachers with ideas for reimagining and rewriting their own workshopping classrooms and curriculum. While this book does provide a specific curriculum and pedagogy for democratic and justice workshopping, the ideas are shared to inspire independent and critical thinking. The suggestions offered are not meant to be prescriptive; they are descriptive. This book endeavors to make planning and teaching for democracy and justice visible. It is a book for teachers who realize the need to teach for change. It is a book to help you and your students through the process. Together, let's rewrite the world.

1

Why and How to Workshop

When it is time for you to leave this school, leave your job, or even leave this earth, you make sure you have worked hard to make sure it mattered you were even here.

—Wes Moore, *The Other Wes Moore: One Name, Two Fates*

Why does it matter that teachers workshop for democracy and justice? Drawing on *Workshopping the Canon*, this chapter reviews reading and writing workshop structures and strategies and reimagines workshopping as a process to grow the knowledge, skills, and dispositions necessary for participating in a democracy. With its emphasis on choice, voice, responsibility, participation, collaboration, dialogue, inquiry, authenticity, agency, and rigor, workshopping fosters democratic conditions in which authentic exchanges can occur around issues of moral, social, and cultural significance. The explanation then expands to workshopping toward justice.

Teachers workshopping toward justice embrace a culturally responsive curriculum and foster a thoughtful critique of society to promote and support agency for social change. To create a more socially just world, we balance critical content with pedagogy that fosters democratic dispositions and skills while raising students' critical consciousness. When teachers workshop for democracy and justice, it matters.

What We Know about Workshopping

A workshop is a metaphor for a particular kind of learning environment that organizes reading and writing experiences in meaningful ways. Richly described and detailed by Atwell (1998), reading and writing workshops create authentic and sustained literacy experiences in classrooms. A workshop is learning and learner-centered, social, and collaborative. Students are empowered to make reading and writing choices. They have access to varied texts; the schedule is predictable, and time is allocated for reading, writing, talking, and listening. Teachers teach focused mini-lessons designed to guide students through reading and writing processes. Processes are valued equally with products; students are assessed through performance on meaningful tasks, and learning is individualized. Expectations are high, but there is room for reflection and confusion as long as a safe learning environment is established, which teachers ensure through structured management.

When designing a workshop classroom, teachers provide opportunities for immersion, demonstration, expectation, responsibility, approximation, employment, and feedback (Cambourne, 1984). Students are immersed in a wide variety of genres presented in whole, meaningful contexts and are provided uninterrupted opportunities for authentic literacy experiences. The teacher demonstrates how they read and write and use their own processes of reading and writing as models for students. In turn, the teacher expects students to respond personally, interpret collaboratively, analyze formally, think critically, and take responsibility for many of their own assignments. The teacher and others, including students, provide feedback on literacy experiences.

More specifically, when we workshop the canon, we immerse students in a wide assortment of texts gathered around a unit focus. We bring together classic and contemporary texts, fiction and nonfiction texts, and texts representing a range of world literatures, historical traditions, and genres, as well as texts representing the experiences of different genders, ethnicities, and social classes. The workshopping classroom encourages transaction with multiple texts through a variety of workshop structures and strategies.

Our reading workshop includes time and opportunity for read-alouds, independent reading, shared reading, close reading, readers theater, response engagements, book clubs, Socratic circles, and a variety of mini-lessons (i.e., how-to, reading, literary, craft, vocabulary, and critical). Our writing workshop interweaves with the reading workshop as students write in response to the unit focus, essential questions, mentor or model texts, and other texts introduced throughout the unit. The writing process is supported through workshop structures including writing plans, mini-lessons (e.g., how-to and craft), independent writing, conferences and/or writing circles, and publishing opportunities.

How Does Workshop Foster Democracy?

One of the primary aims of our schools is to help students develop the knowledge, skills, and dispositions needed to participate in a democracy. When teachers create a workshopping classroom, they establish democratic conditions as students inquire into essential questions, make choices for independent reading, participate in shared and close readings, dialogue during Socratic circles and book clubs, write in varied genres with authenticity, and publish their ideas for the common good. Workshop structures and strategies encourage student response, choice, responsibility, and voice, which prepares students for active citizenship.

More than twenty years ago, Bomer and Bomer (2001) suggested guiding principles to foster a democratic environment, including intention, dialogue, collaboration, and inquiry. Students in a workshopping classroom demonstrate intention as they make reading and writing choices, dialogue as they respond to what they read and write, collaboration as they think and work together, and inquiry as they explore a unit focus and essential questions. Becoming a workshop teacher requires a move away from traditional teaching because practicing skills, memorizing facts, and taking tests does little to prepare students for civic engagement.

Workshopping teachers do not teach in product-oriented, test-centered, top-down ways. Instead, we provide students with choices and foster responsive classroom environments with connections to real-life experiences. A classroom workshop is constructivist because students are active learners who make personal meaning of texts and experiences. Teachers support the development of individual readers and are concerned with how readers make meaning. The processes of reading, writing, and talking about literature are valued as much as the substance of what is read, written, or spoken.

When workshopping F. Scott Fitzgerald's *The Great Gatsby*, for example, students can read, talk, and write throughout a unit focused on the America Dream. Teachers might conduct a shared reading of the core text while supporting student choices with independent reading of young adult novels related to the unit focus. Teachers can read aloud picture books, poetry, and lyrics to prompt response and participation. Students make societal connections as they read informational articles in preparation for a Socratic circle and engage in authentic dialogue with other readers during book clubs with young adult novels. They express their voices as they write a culminating essay, engaging in inquiry around their chosen topic and selecting among an array of genres to represent their ideas. The writing process is supported with time for independent writing and opportunities for talk, collaboration, and decision-making during writing conferences and/or writing circles. Workshop structures and strategies such as these encourage student response, choice, responsibility, and voice, which prepare students for active citizenship.

In accordance with Dewey (1916, 1966), who believed the goal of education is to improve students' ability to understand, articulate, and act democratically, workshopping teachers create classrooms in which students participate and make decisions, taking on responsibilities for the greater good. For this to occur, all perspectives must be welcomed and differences explored. It helps when we guide students to think about classroom life in terms of a participatory democracy. My posted classroom policies and procedures, for example, include guidelines for participation, communication, responsibility, and respect. Each policy and procedure is initially discussed with students, who help to revise and edit the classroom guidelines. In return, my teaching must model fairness, respect, and sensitivity. More specific guidance for facilitating democracy and justice through workshop structures and strategies includes essential questions, reader response, shared and close reading, critical synthesis, Socratic circles, book clubs, writing, research, inquiry, and agency, all of which are discussed in the following chapters.

Teachers who workshop for democracy and justice are working to create a different kind of society—both within the classroom and beyond the classroom doors. As Dewey (1916, 1966) proposed, a curriculum should have "the intention of improving the life we live in common so that the future shall be better than the past" (p. 191). Workshopping for democracy has a moral dimension as both curriculum and pedagogy aim for a greater good. As Goodlad et al. (2004) explain:

> [A] democracy demands a special kind of literacy that goes beyond merely comprehending words on a page or adding up columns of figures. It requires a literacy that includes such skills as critical inquiry; knowing how to ask questions and what kinds of questions need to be asked in a given circumstance; knowing how to evaluate the legitimacy and accuracy of an argument and the data that accompany it, to view issues from a variety of perspectives, and to evaluate the implications of a given text, read between the lines, and recognize and understand the unstated, the omitted, the subtext. In other words, literacy in a democracy is not only a special kind of literacy; it is also a more complex kind of literacy. And because of its uniqueness and its importance, teaching literacy in a democracy has a different kind of moral dimension than, say, teaching literacy under an authoritarian regime. (pp. 8–9)

Teachers workshopping for democracy and justice consider the ethics of their curriculum, pedagogy, and society.

Democracy can serve as a powerful vehicle for dismantling inequities and improving society. So can our workshops! Teachers move beyond basic literacy and interweave critical literacy into workshop structures and strategies in order to workshop the canon for democracy and justice. We re-see read-alouds, independent reading, reader response, shared reading, close reading, literary theory, book clubs, Socratic circles, and independent writing, reimagining structures and strategies to foster in students habits of listening, consideration of perspectives, capacity for collaboration, opportunities for deliberation, respect for others, resistance to discrimination, and development of social agendas. In sum, we reimagine workshopping to foster students' understanding of democracy and democratic processes.

When we embrace our social responsibilities as workshop teachers, we use our reading and writing curriculum and pedagogy to help students craft a better world. We critically examine a unit focus, essential questions, and supporting texts; we use read-alouds and independent reading to provide multiple perspectives; we revise shared reading and close reading to examine issues of power; we teach mini-lessons to read *with* and *against* text; we consider our language use during Socratic circles and book clubs; and we write to develop our public voices for positive change. Workshopping is our means for imagining and realizing a better world.

Workshopping toward Justice

Teachers who workshop for democracy and justice balance pedagogy that fosters democratic knowledge, skills, and dispositions with critical content. We may introduce critical content through new texts we purposefully seek or by re-seeing texts we already teach. Workshopping teachers view texts, structures, and strategies through a critical lens, making needed revisions to curriculum and pedagogy in order to teach for democracy and justice.

Before reviewing what and how we teach, let's review what it means to teach for social justice. Quite simply, social justice is about power—who has it, who doesn't, and why. According to Freire (2013), we can begin to teach for social justice by raising critical consciousness. Critical consciousness, the core of social justice teaching, is a heightened awareness of the world and the power structures that shape it. Our critical consciousness increases as we come to perceive contradictions and oppressions in the world. We learn to notice the difference between those who have power and those who don't, and we ponder the reasons why. We come to notice incongruities and coercions in surrounding societal structures. For example, why do some schools have more resources than others? I have certainly questioned why my school district sent home packets of work for students to complete during the COVID-19 pandemic lockdown while a neighboring district was able to continue classes synchronously online because all students were issued Chromebooks at the beginning of the school year. Critical questions my students have often asked include the following: Why do some schools have better lunches? Why is their football field bigger? Why do I get followed when I'm at the mall? How come she got suspended for only two days for doing the same thing I did, but I got suspended for five days? Or larger societal questions: Why are women more often sexually harassed in the workplace? Why are African American males more often victims of police brutality?

Teachers for social justice structure reading and writing workshops that develop their students' awareness and consciousness. We guide students to become critical observers of the world and text, noting issues of race, gender, class, and difference, prodding them to question issues of power and privilege. Key questions in a social justice classroom include the following: Who benefits? Who is marginalized? Why is a practice fair or unfair? How could it be different? What kind of society would I like to live in, and how can I get there (Golden, 2008)? To grow our students' understanding of racism, classism, and sexism through a close examination of text and life, we critically consider how society perpetuates hierarchies. A critical workshopping pedagogy and curriculum helps students identify, address, and challenge inequity and injustice.

Ultimately, teachers workshopping for justice try to foster in students a sense of agency and capacity to interrupt and change oppressive patterns in themselves and in the world. In short, we teach by raising student consciousness and then trusting that students "will feel increasingly challenged and obliged to respond" to the inequities and injustices they come to recognize and realize (Freire, 2014, p. 81). As Nieto and Bode (2007) explain, we want students to challenge, confront, and disrupt "misconceptions, untruths, and stereotypes that lead to structural inequality and discrimination based on race, social class, gender, and other social and human differences" (p. 11). Agency and engagement are intrinsic to social justice teaching in a democracy because as learners challenge individual and systemic forms of injustice, they also learn how to be active and engaged citizens.

Workshopping can be both a tool for inquiry and a pedagogy of resistance. Let's face it—literacy is never neutral. Why we teach, what we teach, how we teach, where we teach, and who we teach reveal bias. Throughout this chapter and the preceding introduction, I try to clearly articulate why I think it is important to teach for democracy and justice, and I fully acknowledge my own partiality. A teacher's curriculum and pedagogy either sustains or opposes systems of power. We can demonstrate principles of critical democracy and teach for social justice by advocating for texts and teaching that promote critical thinking and support agency for social change. We can use our curriculum and pedagogy to acknowledge, question, and reimagine the world, transforming education and society in the direction of equity and justice.

As we know, "right thinking requires right doing" (Freire, 2001, p. 1). Teachers need to confront systems of oppression through curricular choices and classroom practices. We need examples of social justice pedagogy in the English language arts classroom that alter more traditional forms of instruction, including traditional workshop structures and strategies. For this reason, we want to review and revise what we teach and how we teach when workshopping the canon.

What We Teach

What we teach matters. We know there are valid arguments for and against teaching canonical works. There are those who support the canon and use these texts as a basis for comparison, and there are those who challenge these texts for their "whitestream" (Urrieta, 2009) representations of experience—those who note the absence of African American, Native American, Asian American, and Latinx representation in terms of author or understanding. What we also know is that schools are academically, socially, culturally, and linguistically rich and diverse. Workshopping teachers recognize the need to provide different representations of peoples, societies, mores, backgrounds, traditions, ethnicities, and customs through texts and encourage engagement with cultural and societal issues in literature, literacy, and the world.

Workshopping teachers adopt a culturally responsive curriculum. According to Gay (2010), being culturally responsive entails

> seeing cultural differences as assets; creating caring learning communities where culturally different individuals and heritages are valued; using cultural knowledge of ethnically diverse cultures, families, and communities to guide curriculum development, classroom climates, instructional strategies, and relationships with students; challenging racial and cultural stereotypes, prejudices, racism, and other forms of intolerance, injustice, and oppression; being change agents for social justice and academic equity; mediating power imbalances in classrooms

> based on race, culture, ethnicity, and class; and accepting cultural responsiveness as endemic to educational effectiveness in all areas of learning for students from all ethnic groups. (p. 31)

A culturally responsive workshop curriculum includes relatable, responsive, and relevant texts representative of a wide variety of genres across time periods that explore race, culture, ethnicity, class, and difference and/or confront stereotypes, prejudice, racism, intolerance, injustice, inequity, and oppression.

Teachers workshopping the canon for democracy and justice immerse students in diverse texts, providing multiple viewpoints and an array of representations gathered around a critical unit focus. If teachers choose to teach a canonical literary work, they are purposeful about their choice of the core text, critical in their unit focus, and politic in their essential questions. Workshopping teachers are strategic in their choices of supplementary texts, explicitly seeking out genres representative of students' own groups and language practices as well as those of different groups. We practice structures and strategies leading to democracy, advocacy, and agency. Language is recognized and explored as an instance of power. Research and writing are authentic and focused on change for the betterment of a community.

To demonstrate what we teach when workshopping for democracy and justice, let's revisit the unit previously introduced, focused on the American Dream. As we know, workshopping teachers are purposeful in their selection of a core text. While some may still elect to teach F. Scott Fitzgerald's *The Great Gatsby*, others may select Ibi Zoboi's *American Street* as a cornerstone novel for their unit. Both texts can be used to support a more critical unit focus and essential questions such as, What is the "American" dream? Is the American Dream equally accessible to everyone?

To introduce social justice concepts, workshopping teachers are strategic in their choice of supplementary texts. For this unit, I want to include representative and diverse selections for independent reading, such as Sherman Alexie's *The Absolutely True Diary of a Part-Time Indian*, Sandra Cisneros's *The House on Mango Street*, An Na's *A Step from Heaven*, Sampson Davis, George Jenkins, and Rameck Hunt's *The Pact*, Jeannette Walls's *The Glass Castle: A Memoir,* Sister Souljah's *The Coldest Winter Ever,* and Bryan Lee O'Malley's *Seconds.* I may read aloud picture books, including Walter Dean Myers and Christopher Myers's *We Are America: A Tribute from the Heart*, René Colato Laínez and Joe Cepeda's *From North to South*, Roda Ahmed and Stasia Burrington's *Mae among the Stars*; or poetry such as Tupac Shakur's "The Rose That Grew from Concrete," Langston Hughes's "A Dream Deferred," Ricardo Sánchez's "I Yearn"; or lyrics such as those for The Notorious B.I.G.'s "Juicy," David Bowie's "Young Americans," or Green Day's

"Jesus of Suburbia." In preparation for Socratic circles, we will read articles on immigration policies and economic division that offer multiple viewpoints. Research and writing around these texts will be authentic and lead to change efforts for the betterment of our communities.

How We Teach

How we teach matters. When workshopping the canon for democracy and justice, teachers practice culturally relevant pedagogy which "helps students to accept and affirm their cultural identity while developing critical perspectives that challenge inequities that schools (and other institutions) perpetuate" (Ladson-Billings, 1995, p. 469). We challenge through questioning. When we approach text with culturally relevant and critical pedagogy, we open a space where students have the freedom to question text, self, others, and society.

Through workshopping, teachers model and teach the democratic knowledge, skills, and dispositions needed to discuss issues of justice with diverse groups, build on students' understandings of culture and identity, and formulate questions that guide students' thinking about the authors' assumptions and purposes in the contexts in which the works were constructed (Mantle-Bromley & Foster, 2005, p. 72). We can finally answer Morrell's call (2005) for an increased emphasis on critical English education. A critical English education disrupts existing power relations, deconstructs dominant texts, including canonical literature, and creates critical texts that can be used in the struggle for social justice.

Teachers must ask difficult questions when workshopping for democracy and justice. We question our choice of texts, unit focus, and essential questions. We wonder why we respond to texts as we do. We ponder the use of oral and written language. We interrogate issues of power. And more than anything, we query whether we can do anything about these issues. As we reimagine, revise, and reveal our workshop structures and strategies in the coming chapters, questioning as pedagogy will entwine with reader response, shared and close reading, critical synthesis, Socratic circles, book clubs, writing, research, inquiry, and agency.

None of this will be easy. Questions can lead to discomfort. All of us have squirmed at least once in our lives when asking or answering a critical question. But we need to embrace the difficult. We need to have honest, sometimes painful conversations without being defensive. We can't just gloss over the fault lines that divide us. Instead, we need to "hold them up to the light, honestly confront how they've privileged us and held us back, how we relate to them, how we buck being defined by them but sometimes are anyway" (Older, 2013, para. 8).

It is only our discomfort as adults, our fear of not having answers and solutions, that holds us back. "We are afraid that we won't know what to say, that we will uncover some ugly truths about our communities, about ourselves. Probably, we will." But being "a little bit itchy" (Rhuday-Perkovich, 2017, p. 27) is good for us.

When we ask tough questions, we will get different answers. As we know, different experiences foster different beliefs and values. We can't expect students to share the same ideas as their classmates. Teachers, especially, need to carefully examine their own assumptions before guiding students in a critique of society. Our job is to ask difficult questions and encourage informed responses (and critical reflection on these responses). Through reading, talking, writing, research, and inquiry, students will pursue answers to queries about themselves, each other, and the world that surrounds them. Teachers who practice social justice education help students learn to express themselves as individuals, community members, and global citizens. Yes, teachers may need to negotiate social difficulties. But as Rhuday-Perkovich (2017) encourages, our efforts are worthwhile: "[T]here is *big* magic that can happen when we take it further. When we go from sprinkling our lives with diversity and move to inclusion, from inclusion to justice. To reading the change and being it, to inviting readers to read with empowerment and transformation . . . because it enlarges both our hearts and our souls" (p. 25). Workshopping for democracy and justice matters.

Chapter Summary

This chapter introduces workshopping as a process for democracy and justice. With its emphasis on choice, voice, responsibility, participation, collaboration, dialogue, inquiry, authenticity, agency, and rigor, workshopping fosters democratic conditions in which authentic exchange can occur around issues of moral, social, and cultural significance. Workshopping can also be used to teach for social justice as we heighten students' critical awareness, guiding them to become critical observers of the text and world, noting issues of race, gender, class, difference, power, and privilege, and fostering in students a sense of agency and capacity to interrupt and change oppressive patterns in text, themselves, and the world that surrounds them.

Teachers who workshop for democracy and justice balance pedagogy that fosters democratic knowledge, skills, and dispositions with critical content. We teach for social justice by advocating for texts and teaching that promote critical thinking and support agency for social change, adopting a culturally responsive curriculum and practicing culturally relevant pedagogy. Teachers who workshop for democracy and justice utilize workshop structures and strategies to foster democratic knowledge, skills, and dispositions; teach a culturally responsive curriculum; and practice culturally relevant pedagogy to foster a thoughtful critique of society and promote agency for social change.

2

Planning to Teach

Never let your obstacles become more important than your goal.

—Dashka Slater, *The 57 Bus*

Teachers who workshop for democracy and justice plan and teach toward a greater societal and global good. We foster democratic dispositions and skills while raising students' critical consciousness through curricular and pedagogical choices. To reach our goal of a more socially just world, we carefully design critical content and promote democratic pedagogy.

Chapter 2 provides guidance as you plan for workshopping toward democracy and justice. First, we question the texts we teach, purposefully selecting core works of literature that encourage students to identify, understand, and question systems of power and oppression in society. Next, we select a unit focus related to the core text(s) that fosters justice, equity, democracy, and inclusion. We pose essential questions that encourage us to explore multiple texts and perspectives, examine what it means to be citizens within a democracy, raise critical awareness and consciousness, and encourage social action and change. Last, we interweave diverse and relatable texts, making sure these selections foster real-world connections, share multiple perspectives, include first-person accounts, and offer alternative ways of seeing, viewing, and interacting with the world. These procedures establish a necessary foundation for teaching toward democracy and justice.

Question What You Teach

How do teachers select a text to teach? Do national standards influence the decision? Does the district provide a curriculum guide? Do teachers in the department collaboratively decide on core novels to be taught across grade levels? Are choices based on texts most frequently included on Advanced Placement or International Baccalaureate exams? Or do they make autonomous decisions each year based on student interests and, of course, text availability? Workshopping teachers question why we teach what we teach.

One of the most important political decisions we make as English language arts teachers is deciding what to teach. Yet so often we make these decisions with little awareness that we are teaching—or not teaching—for democracy and justice. Curricular decisions are instead compelled by logistical factors. We should be asking ourselves whether we are making choices that will deepen student understanding of diverse cultures, promote thoughtful democratic discourse around societal issues, and promote analytical thought through critique of the written word. These features of our work are fundamental both to the English discipline and to a democratic society.

The literature we choose to include and exclude reveals whose stories matter. These choices reveal what counts as "quality" literature in classrooms. Beers and Probst (2013) conducted an extensive survey of 2,300 teachers in 2008 and 2010 to determine the most frequently taught books in grades 4–10, and their listing for grades 9–10 includes *1984* (1949), *Adventures of Huckleberry Finn* (1884), *Animal Farm* (1945), *Brave New World* (1932), *The Crucible* (1953), *Fahrenheit 451* (1953), *Frankenstein* (1818), *Great Expectations* (1860), *The Great Gatsby* (1925), *Heart of Darkness* (1899), *Jane Eyre* (1847), *Lord of the Flies* (1954), *Of Mice and Men* (1937), *Othello* (1622), *Pride and Prejudice* (1813), *Romeo and Juliet* (1597), *The Scarlet Letter* (1850), *A Separate Peace* (1959), *Their Eyes Were Watching God* (1937), *Things Fall Apart* (1958), *To Kill a Mockingbird* (1960), and *Night* (1960).

All of these aforementioned texts were published sixty or (many) more years ago. Only three additional works appearing on the list—*The Kite Runner* (2003), *Monster* (1999), and *The Things They Carried* (1990)—were published within the last thirty-five years. All but one text on the list is fiction. *Monster* is the sole contemporary young adult novel. Only five texts were written by women and two by authors of color. Twenty (I'm including *To Kill a Mockingbird* and *Adventures of Huckleberry Finn* but not *Night* or *The Kite Runner* in this count) of the twenty-five most commonly taught novels focus on white characters, their experiences and perspectives. In the infamous Appendix B of the Common Core State Standards for English Language Arts, the exemplar prose texts listed for grades 9–12 include only six (out of thirty-six) fictional works by American authors of color. Eighteen of the twenty-six informational texts listed for English language arts grades 9–12 were written by white men. Sinclair (2018) criticizes this appendix as being "colonized by whiteness" (p. 90).

These lists (and Sinclair) don't lie, and their omissions reveal an uncomfortable truth. There is "an inescapable agenda in traditional English language arts to replace students' language patterns, aesthetic tastes, literacy practices, and composing practices with those of a dominating culture" (Bomer, 2017, p. 12). How can we argue with this fact when twenty of the twenty-five most commonly taught novels in the preceding list focus on white characters, which ultimately positions and privileges whiteness as normal? The most frequently taught texts and those considered "exemplar" in English classrooms are canonical, and the canon represents a cultural construction of knowledge centered on whiteness that institutions deem superior and essential (Worlds & Miller, 2019). We need to recognize and acknowledge that certain texts, and the knowledge of such, have been cast as one of the dominant ways of demonstrating adolescent and adult literacy and examine the role we play in marginalizing other texts and genres. Rather than reinforcing this cultural construction of knowledge, teachers need to question the texts we teach.

When workshopping for democracy and justice, we have to ask ourselves if our text choices propagate culturally colonizing and culturally restrictive classrooms (Bomer, 2017). If we are not critical when planning and teaching, canonical texts can and will perpetuate dominant ideologies about whiteness, gender, heterosexuality, Christianity, and physical and mental abilities, privileging some ways of being while marginalizing others. Instead, we want to interrogate the texts we teach and use our workshops to ensure a more culturally responsive (Gay, 2010) and culturally relevant (Ladson-Billings, 1995) curriculum and pedagogy. We want to be purposeful about advancing justice, equity, diversity, and inclusion through curricular choices.

Select Core Texts Purposefully

With so many texts to choose from, how can we possibly make the best choices? Christensen (2009) suggests we "read the world" and ask ourselves, what do students need to better understand? Teachers committed to democracy and justice search for texts that help us better read society, critique what's happening, and feel empowered to make a change. We find those texts that are enabling, that include characters who have overcome challenges and obstacles to change. Or we select a text that includes characters who have come to a new understanding of the world and the way the world works (Golden, 2008). When making a choice, Buehler (2020) suggests asking, does the book do good work? More specifically, does the book do good work in representing race, challenging heteronormativity, critiquing gender and class, or confronting power? Workshopping teachers search for inclusive and diverse texts that highlight social, ideological, and political issues.

We search for literature to grow students' multicultural understanding, necessary for living within a democracy. Diversity in literature reflects a dynamic intersection of race, ethnicity, gender, sexual orientation, ability, economic condition, religion, and more. Workshopping teachers make conscious and deliberate choices, choosing texts that introduce students to a variety of settings, characters, and situations. After all, reading allows the means to transport ourselves into the lives of others like and unlike us. As a student once so aptly told Wilhelm (1997), "Reading is a way to get inside other people. It's a way to learn stuff that's impossible to learn any other way because you learn from the inside" (p. 35). With the help of literature, we can provide access to all possible ways of being in our classrooms.

In her memorable scholarship, Bishop (1990) wrote of metaphorical windows, doors, and mirrors. Sometimes books offer windows, she explained, through which students view familiar and less familiar worlds. Windows can also be sliding glass doors, through which readers walk and become part of an author's realm. And every so often, when the light is just right, a window becomes a mirror, and magically, readers see their own lives and experiences reflected in the lives and experiences of others. Social justice teachers purposefully select texts that allow students to see themselves and others. While metaphorical windows and mirrors offer a foundation, ultimately teachers want texts to be doors that students walk through—both by entering the author's realm and by engaging with the world in new ways. By encouraging students to engage with the perspectives of others, we hope to inspire them to walk through real doors in the real world to promote change discovered and inspired through reading.

Let's consider the reading list for a self-identified teacher for democracy and justice. Kayla chooses texts, both fiction and nonfiction, purposefully to expose students to multiple world perspectives. During the course of one school year, students in her English I classroom read the following: Jason Reynolds and Brendan Kiely's *All American Boys*, Walter Dean Myers's *Monster*, David Pelzer's *A Child Called "It,"* Laurie Halse Anderson's *Speak*, Sherman Alexie's *The Absolutely True Diary of a Part-Time Indian*, Ishmael Beah's *A Long Way Gone*, George Orwell's *Animal Farm*, John Steinbeck's *Of Mice and Men*, Angie Thomas's *The Hate U Give*, John Boyne's *The Boy in the Striped Pajamas*, and a selection of short stories from Jimmy Santiago Baca's *Stories from the Edge*. All of these core text selections heighten student awareness of issues of power, privilege, inequity, and injustice.

The schools in which we teach are increasingly diverse. To foster students' interactions with a range of ideas and ways of being, teachers need to provide different representations of peoples, societies, mores, backgrounds, traditions, ethnicities, and customs through texts and to encourage engagement with cultural issues in literature, literacy, and the world. Workshopping classrooms are places where students think critically and honor different perspectives, necessary qualities for living within a democratic society. The texts we select need to represent student experiences, provide multiple perspectives, critique the world, and foster critical awareness.

Yes, the literary canon reflects universal themes, including love, death, prejudice, and coming of age, but it is important that we extend our reach for literature beyond the historical scope of the classics to include literature that portrays the vibrant and multicultured lives students bring to today's classrooms. We cannot continue to teach canonical texts without acknowledging their social, political, or cultural implications. For example, canonical texts frequently used to discuss racism (e.g., Harper Lee's *To Kill a Mockingbird* or Mark Twain's *Adventures of Huckleberry Finn*) are set in the past and focus on white characters' experiences. Too often in English class we impose culture, values, practices, and thinking of an adult and past culture. Are there no more current works of literature (e.g., Ibram X. Kendi and Jason Reynolds's *Stamped*) written by authors of color that teachers could use to explore the history and complexities of race relations in the United States? In the spirit of Morrell (2008), teachers who workshop for democracy and justice can create their own more critical canons inclusive of women, people of color, the young, and other groups.

Teachers who workshop for democracy and justice have options. We can read canonical texts in critical ways or we can replace them with current texts that echo similar universal themes. Or we can do both, opting to teach classical and contemporary literature side by side, interrogating the voices across texts, unpacking the similarities and differences between narratives, and considering these in light of current experiences and realities. It *is* possible, although not always easy, to employ canonical texts to do justice-oriented work, and the following chapters include examples of workshopping the canon for democracy and justice. As an alternative, this book also offers ideas for *displacing* the canon, disrupting the dominant narrative with contemporary texts, so the remaining chapters simultaneously introduce examples of workshopping young adult texts for democracy and justice.

Craft a Unit Focus

Once a cornerstone canonical and/or young adult text is chosen, teachers craft a unit focus, centered on current societal issues, that fosters justice, equity, diversity, and inclusion. The unit focus originates from the core canonical and/or contemporary text but is comprehensive enough to include multiple genres, voices, ideas, and perspectives to be explored within an array of critical reading and writing workshop structures.

Serafini (2001) defines a focus unit as a series of literary experiences revolving around a central theme. It encourages us to think more broadly and intertextually. When we workshop for democracy and justice, we interweave the study of the core text(s) with a variety of genres, helping students "read" society and make connections more easily between text and their lives. We want to create a classroom workshop environment that immerses students in a focused unit of study that includes young adult novels, picture books, nonfiction text (e.g., essays, articles, memoirs, biographies, websites, reviews), graphic novels, short stories, films (including documentaries), poetry, plays, lyrics, art, social media (e.g., TikTok, Instagram, Facebook, YouTube, influencers), and social movements.

Teachers consider the focus and purpose for units carefully and critically, always keeping in mind their goal to advance a more just world. For example, Maples and Groenke (2009) explain their rationale for a unit focused on What or Who Is an American?: "[M]y predominately white students were making stereotypical, hurtful comments towards immigrant students—an increasing population at my school. We wanted to find ways to open lines of communication with my students that might encourage them to reconsider their perceptions of people different from themselves" (p. 29). Wolk (2009) has suggested building units around the habits of mind needed for a socially responsible citizenry, including caring and empathy; social problems and social justice; government and the Constitution; power and propaganda; social imagination; historical consciousness and historical empathy; multicultural community; global awareness; war, peace, and nonviolence; and environmental literacy.

Teachers who workshop for democracy and justice create a curriculum that matters, that helps students make sense of themselves, each other, and the world. Inspired by Christensen (2009), workshopping teachers craft a unit focus around key moral and ethical issues of our time: "Writing and talking about these issues—like race, class, gender, and solidarity—takes them out of the shadow world and into the light of day, so students can understand why things are fair or unfair and how to change them" (p. 1). Through units of study, we can teach students how to use their knowledge to create positive change and make a difference in the world.

In *Workshopping the Canon*, I avoided taking a stance on the teaching of classical works so we could find middle ground. In this new book, however, I suggest a critical approach toward teaching canonical texts that is reflected in the unit focus. If workshopping teachers elect to teach a canonical text, they embed this work in a unit focused on key moral and ethical issues that foster justice, equity, democracy, and inclusion.

For example, if I elect to teach Orwell's *1984,* I focus the unit on Freedom of Speech and Expression. At the time this chapter is being drafted, the United States is awash in "alternative facts" and the daily retweeting of history, so there is a need to revisit and re-see this canonical text. Of course, many leaders across time have manipulated truth through language (e.g., Obama's concealment of the National Security Agency's eavesdropping; Clinton's testimony relying on the word *is;* Nixon's handling of the Vietnam War and Watergate), but it seems timely to once again address speech, expression, and their relationship to power in Orwell's text, for a society needs to be free to question, to doubt, to voice, to imagine, and to create without fear of retribution. Unlike the oppressive government of Orwell's Oceania, I want to inspire critical thought and encourage students to be informed citizens and social agents.

Or if I decide to teach Thomas's *The Hate U Give*, displacing Lee's *To Kill a Mockingbird* as a traditional cornerstone text and springboard for discussion of systemic racism, I focus the unit on Voice and Agency. This young adult novel, set against a backdrop of the Black Lives Matter movement, follows Starr as she learns to speak truth to power against the police shooting of her unarmed Black childhood friend. If we want students to become activists in their communities and to promote positive change, we want to inspire them with literary role models and motivating units of study.

When Kelsey and Jenna planned to teach *The Crucible*, they focused their unit around Wrongful Persecution, opting to teach Arthur Miller's fictionalized and dramatized account of the Salem witch trials, which mirrors the societal and governmental prejudice he experienced under McCarthyism, alongside Dick Lehr's *Trell: Nothing but the Truth*, a young adult novel about the daughter of an imprisoned man who persuades a reporter and a lawyer to help prove her father's innocence. Kelsey explained the purpose for the unit focus:

> I hope to move students to see beyond the cry of witchery and determine that corruption or mistreatment of people classified as "other" by society happens throughout history and different societies. I want my students to begin to question how their judicial systems and society treat different groups of people. Students will gain critical consciousness and understanding of how people's perspectives of society and the judicial systems within that society are constructed around their racial, cultural, and socioeconomic status. Students will work to understand the perspectives of different groups of people that they might not relate to, to better understand how authoritative systems of power treat people categorized by society as "other."

Appendix A includes lists of sample unit foci addressing current societal issues. I offer these as description, not prescription. These units are not intended to be replicated in their entirety; they are provided as models to inspire your own unit planning. Some teachers may choose to focus solely on the Holocaust in lieu of a larger unit focused on genocide. Some teachers may choose to focus a unit solely on gender. Some teachers may expand a unit focused on combating anti-Black racism to include racism in all its many faces and forms. These are professional and biased decisions teachers make every day. I purposely include a wide range of canonical and contemporary core text options, including graphics and nonfiction, to generate thinking around multiple planning possibilities. Some of these units and texts are more appropriate for middle school, whereas others are better suited for high school and university classrooms. And by the time this book is published, there will be more current resources to choose from. I trust teachers to know which units and texts are suitable for their school district and student populations. These units also provide critical essential questions.

Ask Critical Essential Questions

Essential questions relate to the unit focus, connect the core text(s) to other genres, prompt critical thinking across texts, accommodate many possible answers, and spark ideas for further inquiry. Traditional essential questions binding units in a high school English class might ask the following: *What is the relationship between love and fate* (Romeo and Juliet)? *How much control do we have over our choices and actions* (Hamlet)? *What is more important, the journey or the destination* (The Odyssey)? *What defines a hero and heroic action* (Beowulf)? *What does it take to survive* (Lord of the Flies)? *Is utopia possible* (1984)?

Teachers who workshop for democracy and justice, however, ask critical essential questions that, in addition to the above criteria, allow for the inclusion of multiple texts and perspectives, explore what it means to be critical citizens living within a democracy, raise students' critical awareness and consciousness, and encourage students toward social action and change. Teachers pose critical essential questions to inspire students to make a better world.

Since my unit for *1984* is focused on Freedom of Thought, Speech, and Expression, I want to heighten students' critical awareness around access to and regulation of freedom of thought, speech, and expression. As Freire once stated, "Freedom without limit is as impossible as freedom that is suffocated or contracted" (2001, p. 96). But where should we draw the line between independence and government? As we come to discover in *1984*, those in power condense and manipulate language to suppress original thought. In what ways are those in power regulating expression within our society and beyond? For what reasons? And what can we do about it? Throughout this unit, I ask students to ponder the following essential questions: *How are freedoms of thought, speech, language, and expression limited? Why might those in power limit freedom of thought, speech, language, and expression? Should we protect freedom of thought, speech, language, and expression? And if so, how?* I encourage students to live the tension and experience the contradiction between freedom and authority with an aim toward social responsibility.

In my unit focused on Voice and Agency and *The Hate U Give*, I want students to explore the complexities of social action and consider what it means to be social activists. Through Thomas's narrative, we follow sixteen-year-old Starr as she witnesses her friend Khalil being shot by the police, cheering as she eventually breaks her silence, gains her voice, and turns to activism. To affect change, we must all act, and I guide students to consider the kinds of action they might take to address the social and political issues raised by the novel. I ask students to consider the following critical essential questions: *When should we use our voice to act against injustice? What is the relationship between voice, agency, and power? How can we gain voice and act against injustice?*

In moving their teaching of *The Crucible* and *Trell: Nothing but the Truth* into the realm of social justice, Kelsey and Jenna guide students to critically analyze the civility of the justice system within their society and societies within pockets of history to determine how communities treat groups of people differently. The essential questions used to develop students' critical thinking include the following: *Who is guilty until proven innocent? Are judicial systems just and civilized? Who is accused, and who are the accusers in society? Whose voices are seen as evidence? Who is more powerful in society, the group or the individual?*

Interweave Diverse and Relatable Texts

After crafting the unit focus and asking critical essential questions, teachers collect diverse and relatable texts, making sure the selections foster real-world connections, share multiple perspectives, include first-person accounts, and offer alternative ways of seeing, viewing, and interacting with the world. To workshop for democracy and justice, teachers select a wide variety of genres that complements the core text(s), expands the unit focus, and helps to answer essential questions. We gather other genres, including young adult novels, short stories, informational texts, picture books, music, art, movies, and social media (e.g., TikTok, Instagram, YouTube, Facebook, influencers). Multiple texts provide more opportunities to immerse students in authentic and critical literacy experiences, increasing student comprehension and motivation while fostering diverse perspectives.

Teachers who workshop for democracy and justice create a curriculum representative of the students we teach. Genres selected are representative of the diverse streams of culture, history, and language that compose today's increasingly global society (International Literacy Association, 2018). Through exposure to multiple texts, teachers offer alternative ways of seeing, viewing, and interacting with the world. We create a compendium of textual voices that exist in dialogue with one another. Whenever possible, we include texts written by primary voices so that students can hear first-person accounts rather than reading others' appropriation of their perspectives.

When a core text is canonical, it is vital that we supplement the unit with diverse texts. Let's consider again *1984*. Listed as the most frequently taught novel in grades 9–10 in Beers and Probst's (2013) survey of teachers, *1984* was written by a white, European male and shares the white, Eurocentric male narrative, a story in which Julia, the primary female character, is both sexualized and pushed to the periphery. While I could certainly include this novel in a unit focused on Freedom of Thought, Speech, and Expression, as previously mentioned, I could also teach *1984* alongside *The Hate U Give* in a unit focused on Voice and Agency to explore the following critical essential questions: *When should we use our voice to act against injustice? What is the relationship between voice, agency, and power? How can we gain voice and act against injustice?* I could introduce other voices and viewpoints with other contemporary text options, including Elizabeth Acevedo's *The Poet X*, Samira Ahmed's *Internment*, Abi Daré's *The Girl with the Louding Voice*, and Jason Reynolds and Brendan Kiely's *All American Boys*. See Appendix A for more extensive lists of diverse text suggestions to workshop this unit and others for democracy and justice.

Appendix A provides lists of multiple genre possibilities that can be used to explore essential questions within a unit focus. While these are extensive, they are certainly not exhaustive listings. As previously mentioned, all texts included reach across middle, secondary, and university classrooms and need to be culled. I have opted to include some informational texts and graphic novels within the heading of contemporary text because they could certainly serve as cornerstone texts or book club options (e.g., Melba Pattillo Beals's *Warriors Don't Cry*, Lorene Cary's *Black Ice*, Tony Medina's *I Am Alphonso Jones*, Marjane Satrapi's *Persepolis: The Story of a Childhood*). Teachers will also notice that certain genres weigh more heavily than others in certain units. For example, in a unit focused on Persecution, I include a larger number of critically acclaimed films.

Some units have more picture books or poetry or informational texts than others. These decisions were based solely on my personal genre inquiry (I watched a lot of Netflix during lockdown).

Teachers who workshop for democracy and justice view supplemental texts through a critical lens. Not all young adult novels are diverse (Thomas, 2018), and we need to search for those books that are inclusive and representative of many ways of being (e.g., class, gender, race, ethnicity, sexual orientation) in this world. We want to consider the beliefs, values, attitudes, social positions, geographies, and experiences represented in the texts we offer students. Myers (2014) specifically urges us to seek out children's books with diverse characters and warns us this will not be an easy task.

There are online resources to help us expand and diversify the curriculum. #DisruptTexts (Ebarvia et al., 2018) is a chat and website developed by English teachers that challenges the traditional canon in order to create a more inclusive, representative, and equitable language arts curriculum. Through Twitter participation, a chat dedicated to a canonical text takes place over a week. During this time, teachers discuss both the value and problematic nature of teaching the canonical work and consider how it could be used to discuss contemporary political issues and suggest additional texts that could be used to disrupt the perspectives and ideologies in the canonical text. The site archives these disruptive conversations.

We Need Diverse Books (https://diversebooks.org/) is a grassroots organization of children's book lovers that advocates for diversity in the publishing industry. The website includes helpful resources on race, equity, antiracism, and inclusion as well as diverse book recommendations. Similarly, Social Justice Books (https://socialjusticebooks.org/) is a project of Teaching for Change, a nonprofit organization committed to creating schools where students learn to read, write, and change the world. This site provides useful booklists, book reviews, and articles. Also a helpful resource, the National Network of State Teachers of the Year (Bassett et al., 2017) created a social justice booklist arranged by grade levels.

Workshopping teachers interweave representational and relatable genres as a means of providing students with more accessible texts, often bridging the gap between out-of-school and in-school reading. We know students are reading more. The juvenile market for print sales of fiction and nonfiction has grown 40 percent in the last decade (Gilmore, 2015). We also know students are posting, liking, snapping, commenting, saving, sharing, and texting. Workshopping teachers bring students' relevant, authentic, and too often secret literacy lives into the classroom. We embrace TikTok. In my unit focused on Freedom of

Thought, Speech, and Expression, I include a series of videos of Feroza Aziz showing a makeup tutorial while criticizing the Chinese government's treatment of its Muslim population. Feroza Aziz's TikTok account was suspended shortly after her videos went viral, leading to speculation on whether TikTok censored political content that might offend the Chinese government. Whenever possible and relevant, include influencers in texts as a way to foster connections. Kylie Jenner, Jeffree Star, and Charli D'Amelio are just a few examples of internet celebrities who have cashed in on their influence and could be included in a unit focused on the American Dream, leading us to critically consider the act of profiting from self-promotion. If the world really is our curriculum, then we need to interweave more social media into that curriculum.

To foster real-world connections and explore critical essential questions tied to moral and ethical issues of our time, workshopping teachers interweave informational texts into each unit. We use nonfiction to foster critical awareness and raise critical consciousness. Nonfiction—including articles, essays, biographies, autobiographies, memoirs, diaries, blogs, hashtags, social media accounts—has a particular power in that the genre can reveal multiple histories, narratives, perspectives, and truths. To make social issues more authentic and immediate for students, we partner literary works with informational texts. In this way, societal connections are fostered. For example, when Kayla reads *Monster*, students concurrently read articles focused on the metaphorical school-to-prison pipeline. When students read *The Absolutely True Diary of a Part-Time Indian*, they read articles related to the actual Dakota Access Pipeline. Or when they read *A Long Way Gone*, they study the United Nations' *Universal Declaration of Human Rights*. In my unit focused on *1984, The Hate U Give,* voice, and agency, we consider movements such as #BlackLivesMatter and #MeToo and #StopAsianHate as nonfiction, social texts demonstrating the power of collective speech and agency.

Appendix A provides select lists of canonical texts and disruptive contemporary texts paired with potential unit foci, critical essential questions, and sample diverse texts to prod your thinking about resources necessary to workshop for democracy and justice. Please note that while Appendix A provides curricular suggestions, these selections are meant solely to inspire ideas for planning your own curriculum to best meet the needs of students in your particular classroom context. And while change begins with planning, diversity in our reading lists is not enough.

Swapping out books on our classroom shelves is not enough. We also need to change how we teach. The remainder of this book introduces critical reading and writing workshop structures and strategies to foster democracy and justice.

Chapter Summary

This chapter describes how to plan for workshopping toward democracy and justice. Planning entails questioning what you teach and selecting core text(s) purposefully. Teachers for democracy and justice make careful and tough choices about what to read, choosing texts that encourage students to identify, understand, and question systems of power, privilege, and oppression in society.

Once a cornerstone canonical and/or young adult text is chosen, teachers craft a unit focus centered on current societal issues that fosters justice, equity, diversity, and inclusion. We pose critical essential questions that encourage us to explore multiple texts and perspectives, examine what it means to be citizens within a democracy, raise critical awareness and consciousness, and encourage social action and change. Last, teachers interweave diverse and relatable texts, making sure these selections foster real-world connections, share multiple perspectives, include first-person accounts, and offer alternative ways of seeing, viewing, and interacting with the world. We gather a variety of genres, including young adult novels, short stories, informational texts, picture books, music, art, movies, and social media (e.g., TikTok, Instagram, YouTube, Facebook, influencers). Appendix A provides a sampling of texts to inspire curricular planning.

3

Fostering Critical Response

AND YOU KNOW
it's weird to know
a person you don't know
and at the same time
not know
a person you know,
you know?

—Jason Reynolds, *Long Way Down*

How well do we really know ourselves or others? While we tend to see the word and the world (see Freire) through the lens of our own experiences, teachers who workshop for democracy and justice help students know themselves, others, texts, and the world better by fostering critical awareness of the personal, cultural, contextual, historical, political, authorial, and ideological factors influencing the creation of text and shaping our responses to text, others, and the world.

Chapter 3 explains why and how to engage students in critical response through read-alouds and independent reading. Critical literacy is introduced as a theory and practice that fosters a questioning stance, prompting reader-consciousness and text-consciousness. Creating an active workshop environment in which students respond both personally and critically to reading is an important goal for workshopping teachers.

What We Know about Reader Response

We know that reading is a dynamic and situated process. It is first a private act, as each reader uses personal experience to make meaning. When reading Harper Lee's *To Kill a Mockingbird*, for example, Amelia shared that being a white, middle-class, self-identified female who grew up in the South helps her relate to Scout, whereas Darius, who moved recently from a large city in New Jersey, admitted that he struggles to connect with Scout, Atticus, Maycomb, and the overall plot of the novel. When reading Angie Thomas's *The Hate U Give*, however, Darius, a Black, self-identified male, revealed that he relates to Khalil, Maverick, Seven, and the Black Lives Matter movement, whereas Amelia connects with Starr's struggles with identity and her relationship with Chris. Both students read the same novels, but their reactions are understandably quite different. Because of prior cultural and social experiences, they respond to the novels' characters, settings, action, and themes differently.

Meaning is variable. As Rosenblatt (1995) famously summarized, a reader "brings to the work personality traits, memories of past events, present needs and preoccupations, a particular mood of the moment, and a particular physical condition. These and many other elements in a never-to-be-duplicated combination determine his [sic] response to the particular contribution of the text" (pp. 30–31). Each reader arrives at meaning through their associative and personal responses, and these responses are shaped by the cultural and social contexts in which reading takes place.

Workshopping teachers engage students in read-alouds and independent reading to support the unit focus, explore essential questions, and expose students to an array of genres. Through reading, we extend our understanding of the world and come to know ourselves and one another better. All texts read aloud or independently deserve response from students, including canonical and contemporary texts, picture books, short stories, social media, articles, essays, poetry, and lyrics.

For example, teachers might read aloud Carmen Agra Deedy's *The Rooster Who Would Not Be Quiet* or "First They Came" by Pastor Martin Niemöller when exploring a unit focused on Voice and Agency, along with Harper Lee's *To Kill a Mockingbird* and Angie Thomas's *The Hate U Give.* Students could be provided choices for independent reading, including Elizabeth Acevedo's *The Poet X*, Samira Ahmed's *Internment*, Abi Daré's *The Girl with the Louding Voice*, and Jason Reynolds and Brendan Kiely's *All American Boys*. As students read individually, teachers prompt reader response, helping students recall experiences and elicit associations.

Teachers can use a wide variety of prompts (Myers, 1988) to foster reader response:

- How does this text make you feel?
- What is the most important word, phrase, or passage you have read?
- Write about a memory or experience that is similar to what you are reading.
- What would you like to know more about?
- Who is your favorite and least favorite character?
- Which character is most like you or different from you?
- If you could change anything in this text, what would it be?
- Describe and explain a familiar (or least familiar) setting.
- What can you learn about your life from this text?
- What do you like and/or dislike about the way the text is written?
- Select a quotation or dialogue that "speaks" to you.
- What would you do if you were a character in the reading?

When workshopping for democracy and justice, teachers especially want to offer prompts like these that draw on students' unique experiences to foster reflection on similarities and differences that shape our reactions to text. Responses can take many forms, including journals, blogs, vlogs, texts, TikToks, Snapchats, tweets, posts, and podcasts. Students can create top-ten lists, articles, and diary entries; host talk shows, dinner parties, and self-help groups; design outfits, lockers, and bedrooms; make playlists, movie trailers, and pic collages; or perform tableaux as a means of demonstrating textual associations. In my classroom, Lori created a playlist (see Figure 1) of songs for characters in Erika L. Sánchez's *I Am Not Your Perfect Mexican Daughter.* When we facilitate reader response, we guide students to explore the range of connections and emotions elicited by a text.

While reader response fosters a personal approach to literature that helps students gain insight into their lives and situations, it can also be limiting. If reader-response theory is practiced only in ways that highlight the life of the reader at the expense of the textual or the contextual, then the theory is diluted. We don't want to emphasize the personal at the expense of the social and political. Know that I am not discounting the importance of personal associations; I am only suggesting the need to expand and question them. If reader response is

Julia:
"You Can't Always Get What You Want" - The Rolling Stones
"Rebell Yell" - Billy Idol
"Float On" - Modest Mouse
"Mad World" - Tears for Fears
"Over the Rainbow" - Judy Garland

Ama:
"9 to 5" - Dolly Parton
"Respect" - Aretha Franklin
"I Will Always Love You" - Whitney Houston
"I'm Every Woman" - Whitney Houston

Lorena:
"Girl on Fire" - Alicia Keys
"Run the World" - Beyoncé
"No Scrubs" - TLC
"Juice" - Lizzo

FIGURE 1. Playlist for characters in *I Am Not Your Perfect Mexican Daughter.*

a transaction, then the text is an equal partner in that transaction. Rosenblatt (1985) herself viewed the text as central to the literary experience: "[I]t should be recognized that an over emphasis on personality moves the discussion out of the realm of a primary concern from the literary transaction and the teaching of literature" (p. 36).

For quite some time, educators have advocated for more critically and culturally responsive versions of reader response, suggesting teachers guide students beyond their initial, personal responses (Bean & Moni, 2003; Morrell, 2005; Park, 2012; Schieble, 2010; Sumara, 2000). After all, reading and responding alone does not offer readers different perspectives or challenge them to think critically. Reader response offers an ideal foundation on which to build critical literacy.

What Is Critical Literacy?

Critical literacy evolved from the Frankfurt school of critical social theory, which asserts that humans can change society through words and actions, maintaining that a more equitable world can be attained through awareness and criticism of injustice. However, Freire's work on critical consciousness and critical pedagogy in the late 1940s is more prominently associated with the roots of critical literacy pedagogy today. Both theory and practice, critical literacy lacks a distinctive instructional methodology, although dialogue is used purposefully as a means of developing critical consciousness.

Teachers who workshop for democracy and justice purposefully heighten students' critical consciousness by raising their awareness of the world and the power structures that shape it. For example, when reading Ibi Zoboi's *American Street* and F. Scott Fitzgerald's *The Great Gatsby* in a unit focused on the American Dream, Jillian and Dallas ask critical essential questions, including *How does a diverse America challenge and change the stereotypical vision of the singular American Dream? Is the American Dream equally accessible? What can we do to advocate for every person's version of the American Dream?* Critical consciousness increases as students read and realize who has more (e.g., access, opportunity, resources, power) and who doesn't and ponder the reasons why.

Let's begin by viewing text critically. No text is neutral. Each reflects the point of view of the author, the text producer. As critical readers, we need to explore the motivation the author had for creating this text. What was the author's purpose for writing? Why did the author choose to write about this topic, in this way? The motivation could have been conscious or unconscious. Either way, texts are positioned, and all texts read aloud or independently need to be viewed through a critical lens. Authors shape particular versions and visions of the world, including class, gender, and cultural groups, for readers based on their own beliefs, values, attitudes, social positions (e.g., age, race, class, ethnicity), geographies, and experiences (Janks, 2014). It is up to us as readers to scrutinize these visions.

But the author's perspective is not the only perspective. Critical literacy disrupts power relations between the reader and the author. Far from passive, critical readers examine text from multiple perspectives and brainstorm other interpretations. Critical literacy encourages readers to analyze the author's message and consider this message from various viewpoints. What does the author want us to believe? How might alternative points of view be represented? Critical readers ask complicated questions about power and analyze factors shaping text and our responses to text.

Workshopping teachers raise reader and text consciousness by questioning the word, by guiding students to think critically about its function, origin, and purpose. We may ask, How are characters represented (e.g., class, race, and gender) in the text? Whose perspectives are shared in the text? Who is speaking? Who is listening? Who is not heard? Asking these questions empowers readers. When reading Harper Lee's *To Kill a Mockingbird* through a critical lens, my students questioned why Atticus speaks so often while Tom is rarely heard. Students wondered about Calpurnia's missing perspective. Students become critical agents as they consider the authorial and the cultural relayed through the work. A critical literacy lens directs readers to see both what is included and what is excluded and encourages them to ponder why. Critical literacy thrives in classrooms committed to democracy and justice as students are encouraged to reconsider everyday assumptions about inequities and injustices, oftentimes disguised as what seems "normal" (Lewison et al., 2002).

Critical literacy encourages readers to question social, historical, political, and ideological forces influencing the creation of text. Think especially about ideological wars between the left and the right and the literary products of these battles. What of *1984* and the socialist (or totalitarian, or fascist, or communist) influence on the construction of this novel? What of McCarthyism and *The*

Crucible? What of *Animal Farm* and the Russian Revolution? Or even *Macbeth*, the witches, and King James I? Students need to consider the belief systems implicit or explicit in text and consider how texts lead us to be sympathetic to the author's position.

Critical readers also contemplate the contextual factors affecting their transaction with a text. For example, teachers might guide students to ponder their own beliefs while reading any of the texts mentioned earlier and weigh how these influence their response and meaning-making. I will never forget how Ashley, a devout Jehovah's Witness, responded to the witches in *Macbeth* and how Valeria, a recent immigrant from Cuba, reacted to Napoleon in *Animal Farm*. Students engaged in critical literacy analyze the social, political, and historical nature of themselves, texts, and contexts, which heightens reader-consciousness and text-consciousness. In this way, teachers foster more critical and active readers who challenge rather than passively accept as they make meaning.

While questioning the word, students question the world, or vice versa. Ultimately, teachers who workshop for democracy and justice guide students to become text critics in everyday life. Students are encouraged to problematize the world, to rethink personal and world assumptions. Only when we begin to read the world can we begin to see its patterns, designs, and complexities and to develop the capacity to rewrite, redesign, and reshape it in our communities' interests (The New London Group, 1996).

Why Teach Critical Response?

While readers make meaning of a text, they are also being "made" by a text. The relationship between reader and text is mutual—each influences the other. A reader's perspective shapes the literary work, but the work also has power to guide the reader's response. Knowing this, we need to carefully examine the influences that shape us as readers and human beings. To help students avoid being manipulated by text, workshopping teachers model how to unpack the authorial, social, political, contextual, historical, and ideological and consider how these position and construct readers. If we challenge these constructions in text, we can also turn the critical lens on ourselves and society. Workshopping teachers help students become more conscious of their identities and experiences as constructed within specific power relations.

Our identities are multiple and shaped by different groups and communities to which we belong. As Shor (1999) so aptly stated, "We build ourselves in a world that is building us" (p. 1). Social categories such as race, gender, class, age, sexuality, nationality, ethnicity, religion, and language produce identity positions, and the ways we respond to text are determined by these social categories—their cultural conventions, rules, or norms. For students to analyze their responses to what they have read, they first need to understand how identities are constructed. Believing this, I begin each school year with a unit focused on Identities and Perspectives (see Appendix A). Through reading, talking, listening, and writing, students consider who they are, how they are, why they are, and who they want to become. Janks (2014) helps students identify their differing identity positions as shaped by different social groups through the completion of a graphic organizer. At the center of a circle is a question: Who are you? Students draw lines outward, filling in their various roles and positions. To foster critical awareness, Janks then asks students to consider the conflicting demands of different positions and to identify the positions in which they feel most or least powerful and contemplate why this is so.

Critical readers interrogate readings and responses and the terms of their production, questioning how and why specific readings and responses are produced. When readers respond to texts and critically reflect on their responses and the responses of others, they grow their understanding of self in relation to others. As Eisenbach and colleagues (2018) affirm, "Once students begin to unpack the way in which their culture speaks to their current view and understanding of the world, they can take a step outside of their own experience to gain greater perspective regarding the lives and narratives of those around them" (p. 35). Students can wonder about the particularity of the different ways we transact with text. Exploring and celebrating different responses helps us recognize the diversity of experience and identity, and respecting difference is vital for democracy and justice.

How to Practice Critical Response

Reader-Consciousness

We know each reader transacts with a text differently, and no student's response is more right than another's. As long as a student transacts with the text, their response is valid, no matter how different it may seem from that of the person sitting beside or across. There may be commonalities, but we do not always need to reach for what is similar or familiar with the text or each other. Differences exist, and we want to foster understanding of and respect for these differences. Teachers begin to foster reader consciousness by growing students' awareness of varied responses. When Lori shared her playlist (Figure 1), for example, students discussed their varied musical tastes. Acknowledging individual differences can lead us to a greater understanding of one another and the world.

Once we become more aware of diverse associations elicited by a text, we are ready to explore what shapes a reader's response and to grow our reader-consciousness. As Rosenblatt states, "When the young reader considers why he has responded in a certain way, he is learning both to read more adequately and to seek personal meaning in literature" (1995, p. 70). To heighten reader-consciousness, I use the following prompt:

- Reread your initial personal response to what you have read. Why do you think you responded in this way? Do you think your response was influenced by your family or friends? By your race, gender, age, socioeconomic status, ability, faith, or sexual orientation? By your beliefs? How do any of these factors affect your response?

Teachers can also raise reader-consciousness by asking students to consider *why* they responded to initial prompts used to foster a reader response:

- How does this text make you feel?
  Why do you think the text makes you feel this way?
- What is the most important word, phrase, or passage you have read?
  Why do you think you selected this word, phrase, or passage?
- Who is your favorite and least favorite character?
  Why do you think you like/dislike this character more than others?
- Which character is most like you or different from you?
  Why do you think you notice these similarities/differences?
- If you could change anything in this text, what would it be?
  Why do you think you want to change this aspect of the text?
- Describe and explain a familiar (or least familiar) setting.
  Why is this setting familiar/unfamiliar?
- What do you like and/or dislike about the way the text is written?
  Why do you think you like/dislike the way the text is written?
- Select a quotation or dialogue that "speaks" to you.
  Why do you think this quotation or dialogue resonates with you?

Workshopping teachers raise the reader's consciousness of the factors that affect their response. So many factors of background and culture shape transactions, and student responses to text reveal beliefs, values, assumptions, and attitudes that derive from certain ideologies.

Not too long ago in my classroom, students were asked to write for ten minutes, selecting from a series of response-based prompts. They were then asked to reread their responses and consider why they responded in that way, and then write about their reasons. In her thinking about her initial response to Simone Elkeles's *Perfect Chemistry*, Alexis wrote: "I think I am feeling this way towards this book because I have had a relationship with someone involved in a gang, so I can relate to this. I can also relate to Brittany because she tries to seem perfect and act happy when inside, that isn't the case." When we layer critical literacy over reader response, readers can critically scrutinize initial responses for their influences, reflecting on the stance they have adopted toward a text, examining their values and roles in society, and ultimately move toward more critical readings.

Critical literacy helps students consider how their social positions—their situatedness and subjectivity—influence their understanding and enjoyment of literary works. This heightened awareness, in turn, can help them become more accepting of their peers' responses as they try on alternative ways of being, comparing similarities and differences with others. We want to help students become more reflexive and conscious of their operating worldviews and examine alternative ways of understanding their world. The more we know about each other's experiences and how these affect understandings, the greater respect we can foster for diversity.

Text-Consciousness

In addition to heightening reader-consciousness, workshopping teachers guide students to critically consider textual properties and contextual features that might influence their reading or response. Drawing from McLaughlin and De Voogd (2004), Rycik and Irvin (2005), Knickerbocker and Rycik (2006), and Borsheim-Black et al. (2014), as well as Beach's (1993) theoretical perspectives on reader response, I use the following prompts to promote text-consciousness with students:

- What do you think the author wants us to think and why? Why do you think the author wrote about this topic in this way?

- What do you already know about this author? What can you guess about this author?
- Do you think the author was influenced by their background when writing this text? Why? How?
- How are characters represented (e.g., class, race, and gender) in the text? Whose perspectives are shared in the text? Who is speaking? Who is listening? Who is not heard?
- Are any voices missing from what you have read? Is there a different perspective that hasn't been shared or included in the text? What do you think should be added to this text, and why?
- Where are you reading? Why are you reading? When are you reading? How are you reading? Are you reading alone or with others? Are you expected to share your reading or responses with others? How do these factors affect your understanding and response?

Workshopping teachers can model critical response during a read-aloud. Share your initial response to a picture book, article, lyrics, poem, or short story. Then think aloud with students. Ask and answer questions that reveal how you heighten your own awareness of factors affecting your meaning-making process.

Teachers who workshop for democracy and justice encourage students to question where their responses come from and to consider personal, cultural, contextual, historical, political, authorial, and ideological factors shaping them as readers and human beings. A heightened awareness of reader- and text-consciousness deepens our understanding of ourselves, others, and the world.

Chapter Summary

All texts read aloud or independently during a unit deserve response from students. While reader response fosters a personal approach to literature that helps students gain insight into their lives and situations, it can also be limiting. But reader response offers an ideal foundation on which to build critical literacy. Both theory and practice, critical literacy lacks a distinctive instructional methodology, although dialogue is used purposefully as a means of developing critical consciousness.

Teachers who workshop for democracy and justice purposefully heighten students' critical consciousness by raising their awareness of the word, the world, and the power structures that shape both. Critical literacy encourages readers to question personal, cultural, social, historical, political, authorial, and ideological forces influencing the creation of text and our responses to text. A heightened awareness of reader- and text-consciousness deepens our understanding of ourselves, others, and the world.

4

Reading *With* and *Against*

It makes me feel like I'm learning a secret code or something. . . . It's powerful[,] . . . knowing how to read words.

—Renée Watson, *Piecing Me Together*

There is power in knowing how to read words. But there is even more power in knowing how to read between words. Teachers who workshop for democracy and justice guide students to read *with* the text as they facilitate meaning-making from the words and *against* the text as they facilitate meaning-making beyond the words.

Chapter 4 addresses the importance of reading both *with* and *against* text through shared and close reading. When a text is visible and shared, students can perceive an author's syntactical and stylistic choices and ponder the effects on meaning. Teachers guide students to read *with* and *against* through workshop structures that include shared strategic reading, literary close reading, and language close reading. These ways of reading (i.e., *with* and *against*) are reciprocal processes. That's the secret code.

What We Know about Shared Reading

During shared reading, students have a copy of the text either projected or placed in front of them. Students follow along silently, seeing and hearing the text as it is read aloud. During a *shared strategic reading*, workshopping teachers model connecting, predicting, questioning, visualizing, summarizing, inferring, and analyzing as they read *with* students.

Teachers engage students in strategies before, during, and after reading, fostering meaning-making through constructive interactions with texts. For example, before and during reading, we want readers to make predictions. To help students anticipate causal relationships about Tony Medina's *I Am Alfonso Jones,* Sara implemented a strategy called Probable Passage (Wood, 1984). She prompted students to select words from the following list—*boy, gun, protests, city, subterranean, spiritual world, brutality, fire, police, family*—and asked them to arrange the words into categories according to their probable function in the novel (see Figure 2). As students organized words into boxes and drafted a "gist" statement, they made predictions about the characters, setting, and plot.

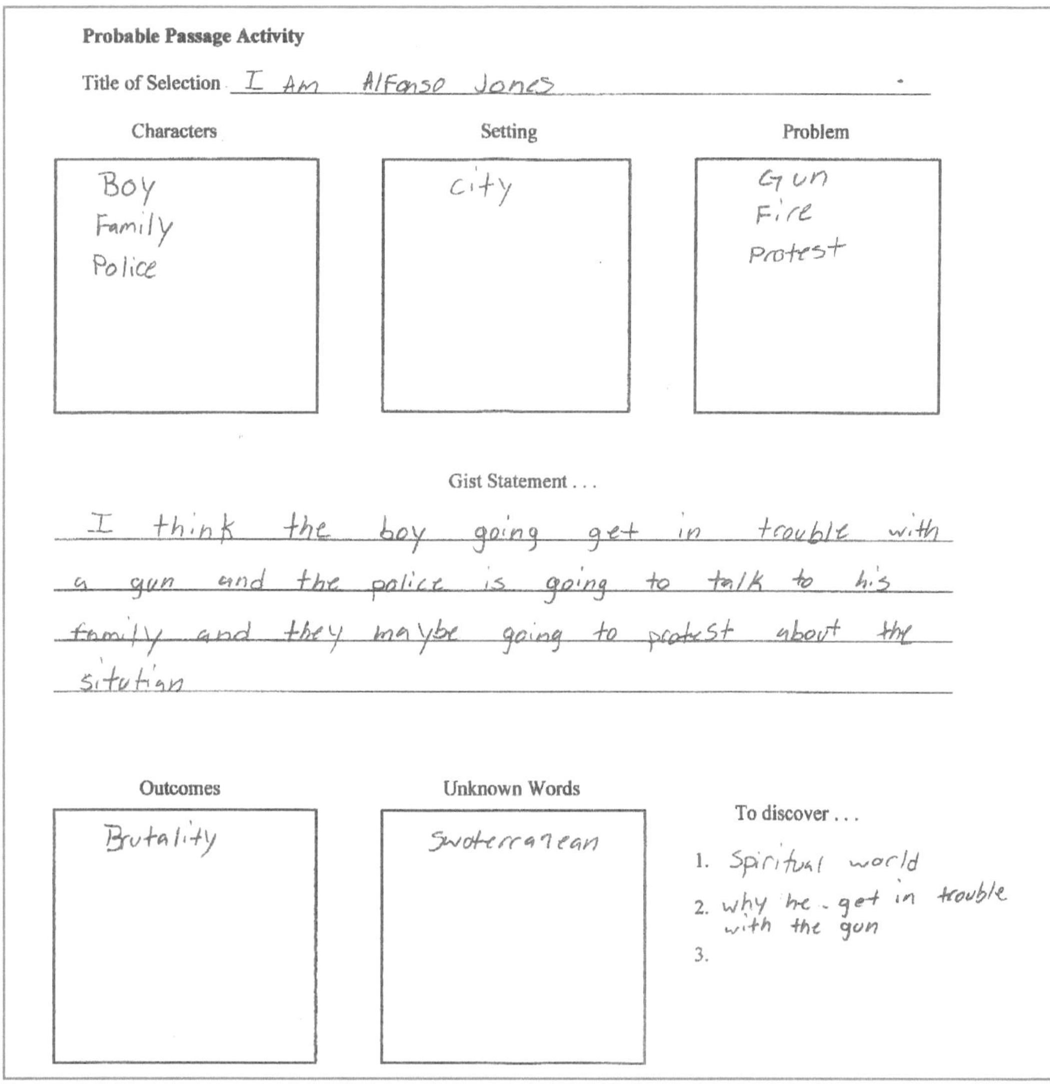

Probable Passage Activity

Title of Selection I Am Alfonso Jones

Characters	Setting	Problem
Boy Family Police	city	Gun Fire Protest

Gist Statement . . .

I think the boy going get in trouble with a gun and the police is going to talk to his family and they maybe going to protest about the situtian

Outcomes	Unknown Words
Brutality	Swoterranean

To discover . . .

1. Spiritual world
2. why he get in trouble with the gun
3.

FIGURE 2. Reading *with* text by prompting predictions with Probable Passage for *I Am Alphonso Jones.*

Along with making predictions, we want students to make connections, relating what they already know to what they will come to know through reading. One of the easiest ways to cultivate connections is with an anticipation guide (Tierney et al., 1995). Helen created a list of ten general statements related to key ideas in Angela Johnson's *The First Part Last* (e.g., *It's important to take responsibility for your actions. Only mothers know how to take care of their children. Your choices define who you are. Only married people can have children.*). Before reading, students were asked to agree or disagree with each statement. Next, they discussed their responses, activating prior knowledge and making personal connections.

Ultimately, comprehending text relies on a student's ability to create images while reading, so we also want to foster visualization. To help students see the action of a text, we prompt them to create visuals to represent understanding. While reading George Orwell's *1984*, Ben sketched a scene from Oceania that included a telescreen, Party Members, Thought Police, and Big Brother.

Students need to query texts. Tovani (2000) encouraged students simply to pose "I wonder" questions. Demetrie wondered, "Why is they protesting?" and "Who is shooting?" while reading Tony Medina's *I Am Alfonso Jones* (see Figure 2).

Along with questioning, students need opportunities to synthesize. Summary challenges students to recap, limit, and organize ideas drawn from a text. Carson used the Somebody Wanted But So strategy (Macon et al., 1991) as a framework for summarizing Ernest Cline's *Ready Player One* (see Figure 3).

Somebody	Wanted	But	So
Wade	to be with Artzmis from the first time they met	he knew he had a mission	Wade tried to balance between the game & Artzmis
the Cataclyst	to kill off everybody	Wade survived (he had an afterlife)	Wade won the game

FIGURE 3. Reading *with* text by guiding summary with the Somebody Wanted But So strategy for *Ready Player One.*

Sometimes it is helpful to provide strategy mini-lessons on relevant structures and features to increase comprehension. When reading Walter Dean Myers's *Monster*, for example, Alex introduced vocabulary necessary for understanding a screenplay. He read aloud a passage of text, highlighting and analyzing structural components, including "cut to," "int," "long shot," and "voice-over."

Finally, inferring involves drawing conclusions or making interpretations about what isn't explicitly stated. When I was reading Angie Thomas's *The Hate U Give*, I used one of my favorite methods for guiding inference, Beers's (2003) It Says—I Say (see Figure 4), which helped students organize their thoughts and connect what is stated explicitly in the text with what is not stated in the text.

Shared reading encourages a text-based approach to the teaching of comprehension-oriented cognitive reading strategies. Through shared strategic reading, teachers model how they make meaning by connecting, predicting, questioning, visualizing, summarizing, inferring, and analyzing. Workshopping teachers guide students to read *with* text by teaching strategies that encourage comprehension.

Question Write down any question you have about what you have read.	**It Says** Find information from the text that will help you answer the question.	**I Say** Write down what you already know about that information.	**And So** Combine what the text says with what you know to come up with the answer.
Why Khalil got to get shot?	"Khalil breaks a rule- he doesn't do what the cop wants." (p. 21)	There are rules we got to follow when police pull us over.	Khalil didn't know the rules or didn't think he should follow them (not fair)

FIGURE 4. Reading *with* text by making inferences with the It Says—I Say strategy for *The Hate U Give*.

What We Know about Close Reading

Close reading is directly related to shared reading. While the definition for close reading varies on particulars, the general process directs students to notice the elements of style and structure an author uses to relay meaning. Beers and Probst (2013) describe the close reading process as working with a short passage; exploring the significance of words, sequence, characters, connections, etc.; extending from that passage to other parts of the text; encouraging exploratory discussion; and rereading with purpose. This detailed course of action fosters close reading.

Close reading asks readers to unravel not just what the text says but also how the text works. When I want students to observe something intriguing about the way a text is written, I stretch a shared reading into a close reading and direct attention to a specific passage of text, guiding students to contemplate how and why a particular character is portrayed or how and why a specific literary device is used. This *literary close reading* encourages students to study the literary technique of the text and consider the author's purpose, discussing and comparing observations as a class, expanding the discussion from the passage to other parts of the text, and finally rereading with new insight.

For example, when reading Nic Stone's *Dear Martin*, Ashley conducted a literary close reading of the following passage: "His eyes drop to the watch. Which puts a big-ass lump in his throat. There's no talking past it, so he does the only other thing that makes sense. He stretches out his wrist and puts it on" (p. 137). Ashley's literary close reading focuses on the symbolic nature of the watch given to Justyce:

> Throughout the story so far, Justyce is constantly reminded of his encounter with the officer that put him in cuffs when he was trying to help Melo out. Whenever he thinks about the incident, or something happens that hits too close to home, Justyce's attention is drawn to his wrists. The bruises from the handcuffs took a while to fade away and Justyce is constantly rubbing them. I believe that his wrists are a big trigger for him and that they are an unfortunate reminder of his encounter with the officer.
>
> After Manny died, his parents have Justyce over for dinner and give him a gift they were going to give Manny. It was a watch that was passed down in Manny's family to the first-born son for decades. The initials inscribed inside are EJR—Manny's great-grandfather's initials and Manny's as well.
>
> I think it is symbolic for Justyce to be gifted something that will go on his wrist. Not only is it a constant reminder of his best friend, but I think it is also a constant reminder of the white cop that killed him. The watch will cover the

> ghosts of the bruises from the handcuffs that haunt Justyce. However, I think that the watch will be a new ghost that will also haunt him. Instead of the handcuff marks that will always connect Justyce to the cop, I think that this watch will always connect Justyce to Manny and the unfortunate incident that caused his death.

Along with concentrating attention on the literary, we can use close reading to guide a reader's attention to the language convention, style, or use evident in a particular text. When conducting a *language close reading*, a teacher draws on a sentence or passage from a text to deliberately guide students' attention to the author's grammatical, mechanical, or usage choices. For instance, a teacher can guide student attention to Angie Thomas's use of dialect in *The Hate U Give*, Martin Luther King Jr.'s use of parallelism in "I Have a Dream," or Nic Stone's change of fonts in *Dear Martin*. While the teacher can preselect and direct students' attention, I encourage students to collect their own language for close reading. We want students to identify unknown vocabulary, discern sentence structure, notice artful parallelism, and observe punctuation independently. If students gather words during an initial shared reading, for example, we can then explore and discuss the significance of diction during a language close reading.

Close reading supports a holistic approach to the teaching of vocabulary, grammar, and literary devices. In the workshopping classroom, we use the structure of close reading to demonstrate language (e.g., conventions, usage, and vocabulary) and teach literary elements (e.g., allusion, conflict, irony, foreshadowing), integrating the study of language with the reading of literature.

Reading *With* and *Against* All Texts

So what do shared and close reading have to do with reading *with* and *against* text? Teachers who workshop for democracy and justice read *with*, deepening student understanding of a unit focus and essential questions through reading multiple genres. We read *with* as we explore a justice-oriented curriculum. Through the juxtaposition of multiple texts, we are able to hear varied viewpoints and gain deeper insight on a topic or issue relevant to teaching for democracy and justice.

Workshopping teachers practice shared strategic reading, literary close reading, and language close reading as demonstrated earlier to enhance student meaning-making. During a shared strategic reading, students read *with* as they connect, predict, question, visualize, summarize, infer, and analyze text. Students read *with* during a literary close reading as they consider the effects of literary elements and techniques on text and meaning. During a language close reading, students read *with* as they deliberate an author's grammatical, mechanical, and usage choices. Students need to be able to read *with* in order to make meaning from the written word, unit focus, and essential questions.

Teachers who workshop for democracy and justice also guide students to read *against* text. The process of reading *against* encourages readers to see underneath, between, behind, and beyond the text. Workshopping teachers view texts as representations of the world, meant to be explored, challenged, and even rewritten, so we look for the ways and means by which texts establish and use power over us and others, considering and contemplating on whose behalf and in whose interest (Molden, 2007). Just as shared strategic reading, literary close reading, and language close reading can facilitate reading *with* text, these same workshop structures and strategies can promote reading *against* text.

Teachers who workshop for democracy and justice appropriate shared and close reading structures and strategies for teaching students to read *against* text. We can use shared reading strategies such as inferring, questioning, visualizing, predicting, connecting, summarizing, and analyzing to examine issues of power, normativity, and representation in text. We can employ literary close reading to critically consider how characters, plot, theme, symbols, or metaphor reinforce and/or challenge issues of power, normativity, and representation. We can also use language close reading as we examine how an author's choice of words or punctuation can be used to manipulate readers and assert the author's intentions and beliefs. Through shared and close reading structures and strategies, workshopping teachers can guide reading *against* and help students identify and understand how text and language are ideological.

Which texts do we read *against*? Teachers who workshop for democracy and justice guide students to read *against* all genres. Of course, it is most vital that we challenge traditional literature, knowing as we do that the canon represents a cultural construction of knowledge centered on whiteness. Shakespeare's plays are an especially ripe field for social justice pedagogies, and Gatta (2019) suggests that teaching students how to read *against* them could be considered a form of activism.

While we make efforts to read *against* the canon, we also want to recognize the complexity in young adult literature and read *against* this genre as well. Although some might not see purpose or value in reading *against* texts that provide needed and missing perspectives and voices, it is important for readers to recognize the power of the author in shaping both the text and the readers of young adult novels just as much as they might for canonical texts. Samira Ahmed, Jason Reynolds and Brendan Kiely, and Angie Thomas were just as purposeful in their crafting of *Internment*, *All American Boys*, and *The Hate U Give*, respectively, as Arthur Miller, George Orwell, and Mark Twain were in their writing of *The Crucible*, *Animal Farm*, and *Adventures of Huckleberry Finn*, respectively. Our student readers can critically analyze a text and their meaning-making processes through shared and close reading structures and strategies.

Students need to think *against* all that they read and see. Both language and image can be manipulated and used to manipulate. Because our units include a wide variety of texts, workshopping teachers can guide students to read *against* visual content, including photographs, graphic novels, film, political cartoons, and art. We can prompt students to consider what or who they see and don't see; how they see and don't see; and why they see and don't see. For example, in a unit focused on Civil Rights, I had students examine a variety of photographs taken during the Birmingham campaign and scrutinize the following: How are protestors and police represented? How does the subject, angle, lighting, or color affect your reading of the photograph? Did different media outlets such as the *Birmingham News*, *Montgomery Herald*, *Atlanta Constitution*, *New York Times*, and *Life* choose to print different photographs? Why? Or when students read a graphic novel such as Marjane Satrapi's *Persepolis*, teachers can ask, How are characters portrayed? What are characters' facial expressions and body language? What is each character doing? Do characters appear to be drawn differently? Why might this be? Are speech bubbles or captions used to show someone speaking? Is the style, shape, or placement of the writing significant? How is the author or artist using this genre to get their point across to readers? Inspired by Janks (2014), we want to read *against* both word and image.

In the following sections, I demonstrate how we can implement shared strategic reading, literary close reading, and language close reading to read *against* a variety of texts.

How to Read *Against* Text Using Shared Strategic Reading

Reading *against* challenges readers to search for what the text says implicitly. When we read *against* text, we are "reading between the lines to expose and interrupt embedded, dominant narratives, power dynamics, and perceived normalcy espoused by and hidden in the text" (Borsheim-Black et al., 2014, p. 125). When we workshop for democracy and justice, we model and share our processes of reading *against* with students, making the implicit more explicit.

A reading strategy such as inferring naturally fosters reading *against* because readers are guided to draw conclusions or make interpretations about what isn't explicitly stated in the text. As mentioned earlier, when I was reading Angie Thomas's *The Hate U Give*, I used Beers's (2003) It Says—I Say strategy (see Figure 4) to help students connect what is stated in the text with what is not stated in the text. While Anya made a text-driven inference by claiming, "Khalil

Question	It Says	I Say	And So	Why?
Write down any question you have about what you have read.	Find information from the text that will help you answer the question.	Write down what you already know about that information.	Combine what the text says with what you know to come up with an answer.	Why do you think the author wants you to think this?

FIGURE 5. Reading *against* text with It Says—I Say—And So.

didn't know the rules or didn't think he should follow them," I could further their critical thinking by adding an additional column to the graphic (see Figure 5). By posing the question, *Why do you think the author wants you to think this?*, workshopping teachers encourage students to analyze the author's message. What does the author want us to believe? And why?

Another reading strategy that supports reading *against* is questioning. While active readers monitor their comprehension as they read *with*, wondering, *Who said that?* or *What did that mean?*, questioning can also be used to challenge a text. If we don't question a text, it can deceive and delude rather than enlighten and expand our knowledge. As discussed in Chapter 3, no text is neutral, and all text must be subjected to interrogation.

Although we want students to scrutinize and query text on their own, it is helpful to model questioning that prompts reading *against* during a shared reading. Not too long ago, I projected and read a passage aloud from Harper Lee's *To Kill a Mockingbird*:

> "Doesn't make it right," said Jem stolidly. He beat his fist softly on his knee. "You just can't convict a man on evidence like that—you can't!"
>
> "You couldn't, but they could and did. The older you grow the more of it you'll see. The one place where a man ought to get a square deal is in a courtroom, be he any color of the rainbow, but people have a way of carrying their resentments right into a jury box. As you grow older, you'll see white men cheat black men every day of your life, but let me tell you something and don't you forget it—whenever a white man does that to a black man, no matter who he is, how rich he is, or how fine a family he comes from, that white man is trash."
>
> Atticus was speaking so quietly his last word crashed on our ears. I looked up, and his face was vehement. "There's nothing more sickening to me than a low-grade white man who'll take advantage of a Negro's ignorance. Don't fool yourselves—it's all adding up and one of these days we're going to pay the bill for it. I hope it's not in you children's time." (p. 223)

After I read, I asked a series of questions drawing from Borsheim-Black et al. (2014, p. 126), including *Whose story is emphasized or valorized? Portrayed as a victim or hero? Is there a different perspective that hasn't been shared or included? What does the author want us to think? How/Does the plot and theme support or challenge normative ways of thinking about topics being portrayed (e.g., racism)?* Together, my students and I cross-examined the text.

We want to guide students to ask complicated questions about power, perspective, and the personal, contextual, historical, cultural, and ideological factors shaping text and our meaning-making processes. McLaughlin and De Voogd (2004) offer a series of critical questions for us to consider modeling, including: *Whose voices are heard and whose are silenced? Who is privileged and who is marginalized in the text? What does the author want us to think? How does the author use specific language to promote their beliefs? What action might you take based on what you have learned from the text?*

Once students are familiar with questioning *against* text, we can trust them to query one another. Before a book club meeting, I ask students to bring three questions with them. Katie asked, "What is the author's purpose in using Starr as the narrator?" when reading *against The Hate U Give.* And Michael asked, "Does the depiction of Layla's family as middle class and educated support or combat stereotypes of Muslim Americans?" while his book club read *against Internment.* We know authors purposefully and powerfully shape their texts, and it is up to us to question the status quo.

Strategic reading *with* a text can lead us to reading *against* a text. For example, I mentioned earlier that Ben sketched a scene to further his meaning-making when reading George Orwell's *1984.* After all, reading is seeing, Wilhelm (2004) reminds us. Once story worlds are rendered, however, we can view them critically. Park (2012) suggests we analyze readers' mental images and visions of settings and situations that can reveal students' identities, subjectivities, or worldviews and can prompt meaningful discussions on race and gender. How did Ben choose to represent Party Members, Thought Police, and Big Brother? Are they male? Are they white? How old do they look? What class and cultural groups do they appear to represent? What does this image reveal about the student artist's beliefs, values, and attitudes about power? How is the status quo supported or refuted in the text or in Ben's drawing? We know authors shape particular versions and visions of the world for readers based on their own beliefs, values, attitudes, social positions, geographies, and experiences, and we can either read *with* or *against* them.

We can reconsider our predictions, connections, and summaries in much the same way. Before reading Tony Medina's *I Am Alfonso Jones,* Demetrie anticipated, "I think the boy going get in trouble with a gun and the police is going to talk to his family and they maybe going to protest about the situation" (see Figure 2). Teachers who workshop for democracy and justice can guide students to reflect critically on their predictions. We could ask Demetrie: Why do you think the boy is going to get in trouble with a gun and not the police? Why do you think the family is going to protest and not the police? What do your predictions reveal about what you think is normal? About who holds power? About who has to protest? Why do you think the author wants you to think about this? Teachers can have students write two gist statements: one for themselves and one for the author.

Helen used an anticipation guide (Tierney et al., 1995) to foster connections before reading Angela Johnson's *The First Part Last*. Students either agreed or disagreed with statements including *Only mothers know how to take care of their children*, *Your choices define who you are*, and *Only married people can have children*. After students initially express their opinion on each statement, teachers can guide students to consider these statements from multiple points of view, asking, Why might someone agree or disagree with this statement? What is the belief system you hold, and how might it differ from others' and the author's? To foster thinking around multiple points of view, I have created a new format for an anticipation guide (see Figure 6). In this way, students can begin to read *against* their own connections.

Students can read against their summaries in much the same way. A summary reveals what students take away from a reading (see Figure 3). When we read *against* a summary, we guide students to consider what they left out and why. After students complete the Somebody Wanted But So activity (Macon et al., 1991), I ask them to review what they have written. Then I ask them to draw two more boxes at the bottom and fill in the following: I left out_______ . I left out _______ because _______. I want students to consider what or who they see as unimportant and to contemplate why.

Authors structure texts purposefully. When we read *against*, we consider how the author's purpose for writing (i.e., to inform, explain, illustrate,

Statement	Agree/Disagree	Why I Agree/Disagree	Why Someone Else Might Think Differently

FIGURE 6. Reading *against* text using an extended anticipation guide.

entertain, explore, persuade, or a combination thereof) affects their decisions about what to include in the writing, such as context, language, and structure. How does the writer want us to see the content from their point of view? How is the story angled to manipulate the reader into that point of view? How does the author use the text to make us understand in a particular way? Let's again consider Walter Dean Myers's *Monster.* Alex introduced vocabulary necessary for understanding a screenplay *with* students. If we want students to read *against* the structure, we can ask, Why do you think Myers chose to write this story in the form of a screenplay? What are the effects of his use of screenplay vocabulary? Does Myers's structure of a screenplay manipulate readers in any way? Why or why not?

Teachers who workshop for social justice flipflop reading strategies to read *with* and *against* text. We use inferring, questioning, visualizing, predicting, connecting, summarizing, and analyzing to examine and expose issues of power, normativity, and representation in texts and in our own meaning-making processes. Through shared strategic reading *against*, teachers can model and share how they make meaning beyond text.

How to Read *Against* Text Using a Literary Close Reading

Workshopping teachers guide students to read *against* text with a literary close reading. As we know, a literary close reading *with* text encourages students to carefully consider the author's use of story elements, figurative language, and/or literary devices in a passage of text. However, when conducting a literary close reading *against* text, students not only note the author's use of technique, but they also critically interrogate how and why certain techniques are used, considering the author's purpose and power in shaping readers' perceptions of normalcy.

Teachers who workshop for democracy and justice engage students in the close reading process as a means of resistance, eventually leading them to question and critique dominant literary and cultural ideology presented in a text, encouraging students to read *with* and *against* their own belief systems and to scrutinize cultural values proffered through story elements (e.g., plot, character, setting, point of view, tone, style, theme), figurative language (e.g., simile, metaphor, personification, alliteration, onomatopoeia, hyperbole, idiom), and literary devices (e.g., allegory, allusion, irony, symbol, imagery, foreshadowing, rhyme). Workshopping teachers want students to recognize and resist dominant literary and cultural ideology.

To engage students in a literary close reading against characters, for example, workshopping teachers focus attention on a passage of text that includes character descriptions and then guide students to consider the following: How are characters portrayed? Consider the author's representation of sex, race, gender, ethnicity, class, religion, ability (physical, mental, intellectual, emotional), sexual orientation, etc. Does the author use stereotypes? Who is left out? Who is the protagonist? The antagonist? Who holds power? Why do you think the author represents characters in this way? Imagine engaging students in a literary close reading against the pilgrims in Chaucer's General Prologue to *The Canterbury Tales*. Or envision a close reading against Hester Prynne, Reverend Dimmesdale, and Roger Chillingworth in Nathaniel Hawthorne's *The Scarlet Letter*.

To foster further close reading against characters, have students "switch" (McLaughlin & De Voogd, 2004) elements of internal or external characterization. To help students realize the biases in the text as well as the author's intentions, have students swap the sex or practice race bending (Owens, 2017) of a main character and reboot the text. Along with revealing an author's mindset, recasting characters using alternative sexes, races, and ethnicities is a form of restorying, which allows texts to be told from new and underrepresented perspectives.

For example, when reading Jason Reynolds and Brendan Kiely's *All American Boys*, my students were told to switch a character's race, gender, sexual orientation, religion, or socioeconomic status. I then asked: How might this story be different? Franny responded in her reading blog:

> The main character of this story (at least so far) is Rashad. Rashad is a Black boy in high school who makes decent grades and stays out of trouble. Or, at least, he tries to. The scene where Rashad gets arrested outside of Jerry's is the perfect example of how the story would be completely different had he been any other race, but for my example, I'm going to discuss how it would be different if he were White. Rashad had just finished explaining how he never steals because he is too afraid of what his dad would do to him. So, we already knew that his intentions were not to steal when going into the store. That is the beauty of first person narration. However, that's what the store clerk didn't know, and he was probably in search of a fight. Had Rashad been White, he would've likely been able to steal a bag of chips without getting caught. What's even worse is, had he been White, he would've been able to have his bag wide open, regardless of whether he intended to steal something or not, and the clerk likely wouldn't have bat an eye at him.

We can apply the same process when engaging in a literary close reading against point of view. Readers can reimagine perspective as well as time, place, mode, metanarrative, and identity, inscribing themselves into existence through retold stories (Thomas & Stornaiuolo, 2016). Teachers can focus student attention on a passage of text and guide them to consider the following: *From whose point of view is the story told? Whose point of view is missing? How might this story be different if we added or switched a point of view?* Ashley reconsidered point of view when reading *All American Boys* and blogged:

> The point of view that is being expressed is Rashad's & Quinn's. We are seeing the point of view of the victim of police brutality & that of an outsider who witnessed the event—one black & one white. The perspective that is missing would be that of the officer who beat Rashad—Paul. So far we know that the officer is Guzzo's older brother & that Quinn looks up to him, but we don't get direct information from him. I think that the story would be incredibly different if we had Paul's perspective alongside Rashad & Quinn's. I think it would be interesting to know how Paul feels. Does he regret what he did? Does he think his actions were justified? Is he scared of a trial? Is he confident that Rashad will go to jail?
>
> There's a part of me that wonders what the reader's reaction would be if we only got Paul's perspective. Would the intention of the author be to get sympathy for the cop? I think if someone wrote that story in today's climate, it would not be accepted well. However, it would be interesting to know the legalities of the trial from the officer's perspective & how their actions effect their family & friends.

To encourage students to consider alternative perspectives, have students write in a new point of view. For example, how might readers challenge representation, normativity, and power by adding Tom's or Calpurnia's point of view to Harper Lee's *To Kill a Mockingbird*?

Workshopping teachers guide students to close read and critically question plot (e.g., How does the plot support certain belief systems or ideas of normalcy?) or theme (e.g., How does the theme support or challenge normative ways of thinking?). When scrutinizing figurative language and literary elements, we ask students not just to consider the effects of literary techniques on meaning, but also to contemplate whether the figurative language and literary elements reflect a particular cultural knowledge. What does a reader need to know in order to understand the symbol, simile, allusion, metaphor, allegory, or irony in the text? What does the author presume readers know? What does this reveal about the author? Close reading *against* empowers readers to recognize, question, and resist an author's literary or cultural ideology.

How to Read *Against* Text Using a Language Close Reading

When conducting a language close reading *with* text, students consider an author's grammatical, mechanical, and usage choices and their outcome for the reader. When conducting a language close reading *against* text, workshopping teachers not only encourage students to unravel an author's techniques and conventions, but also guide them to understand that language and texts are biased. Authors carefully and purposefully sway readers' opinions of people (characters), places (setting), things (plot), and ideas (theme). There is power in language, and workshopping teachers deconstruct an author's language decisions to expose how language can be used to manipulate readers.

Words hold power, and those who have power over words control the narrative. If we consider the text of Shakespeare's plays, for example, we have to acknowledge the power that editors have wielded over the years in shaping the Bard's narratives. Over time, editors have interpreted the text differently, and their own experiences have either informed or perhaps misinformed their interpretations of the plays (Gatta, 2019). Like editors, authors exert power over the narrative through their word choices.

To conduct a language close reading against diction, workshop teachers can focus readers' attention on a passage of text such as the following from Act I of Henrik Ibsen's *A Doll's House*:

HELMER. Is that my lark twittering there?

NORA. Yes, it is.

HELMER. Is it the squirrel skipping about?

NORA. Yes!

HELMER. When did the squirrel get home?

NORA. Just this minute.

Workshopping teachers guide students to critically consider the author's word choices, including *lark*, *twittering*, and *squirrel*. To prompt close reading *against*, teachers might ask: How does the author's word choice affect your perception of Nora? Of Helmer? Of Ibsen? Does the playwright's word choice support or challenge normative ways of thinking about gender? Teachers who workshop for democracy and justice might ask students to switch out words, replacing language to expose bias. What if the author had substituted *hawk* for *lark*? And the hawk was *staring* instead of *twittering*? What if the author substituted *wolf* for *squirrel* and *prowling* for *skipping*? How might this change your perception of

Nora, Helmer, and Ibsen? How is Ibsen manipulating you as a reader with his word choices? Students discuss and apply their findings to different passages, questioning authorial intent through the close reading process.

Workshopping teachers can conduct a language close reading *against* dialogue, guiding students to carefully consider the relationship between power and language. Inspired by Janks (2014), teachers and students might cross-examine an excerpt of dialogue, noting, Who gets to speak? How often? Who speaks for whom? Who interrupts? Who gets heard? Who makes statements, asks questions, or gives commands? Why? Through close reading, students discuss and compare their conversational observations as a class, expanding their discussion from a passage of dialogue to other parts of the text, eventually rereading with renewed understanding.

To engage students in a language close reading against dialect, we follow the same process described above but focus students' attention on the author's use of vernacular. Teachers prompt students to note vocabulary, pronunciation, and grammar. To foster reading *against*, workshopping teachers might ask, Who speaks in dialect? Why do you think the author chooses to use dialect? How does the use of dialect affect you as a reader? How does the author's use of dialect challenge dominant language and cultural norms?

While teachers can guide students' attention to passages demonstrating powerful language choices when conducting a close language reading *against* text, ultimately we want students to identify grammatical, mechanical, and usage choices and ponder their outcome independently. For bellwork, I had students consider crafting techniques and their effects in novels they were individually reading:

> Open your book. Thumb through the pages and notice how it is written. I know this is kind of weird. Instead of focusing on what is written, try to focus on **how**. For example, does the author write dialogue in a particular way? Choose particular words? Do they repeat words or ideas? Construct sentences in certain ways? Punctuate a certain way? What can you notice about the writing style or structure? Once you figure out what they are doing, **why** do you think they are doing this? Is the author trying to achieve some sort of effect (on you as a reader) by writing in this way? Write down your notes, which need to fill half a page of paper toward a classwork grade.

Once students have made their initial observations, I have them gather with book club members who have read the same text:

> Share what you noticed about how your novel is written. Did you notice anything in common? What could you call this? Why do you think the author does this? Consider how the author's purpose for writing (i.e., to inform, explain, illustrate, entertain, explore, persuade, argue, or a combination thereof) affects their decision to include certain elements in the writing such as the language and structure. How does the writer want us to see the content from their point of view? How is the story angled to manipulate us (readers) into that point of view? How does the author use language to make us understand in a particular way?

Workshopping teachers conduct language close readings *against* text so that readers will not only notice how the text is written but will also contemplate why the author made certain writerly decisions. Authors make specific grammatical, mechanical, and usage choices, and we want students to recognize and realize how these choices shape readers and their meaning-making. Teachers practice close reading *against* to expose the relationship between language and power.

Chapter Summary

Workshopping teachers practice shared strategic reading, literary close reading, and language close reading to enhance student meaning-making *with* text. During a shared strategic reading, students read *with* as they connect, predict, question, visualize, summarize, infer, and analyze text. Students read *with* during a literary close reading as they consider the effects of literary elements and techniques on text and meaning. During a language close reading, students read *with* as they consider the grammatical, mechanical, and usage choices made by authors. Students need to be able to read *with* in order to make meaning from the written word, unit focus, and essential questions.

Teachers who workshop for democracy and justice also guide students to read *against* all genres. The process of reading *against* encourages readers to make meaning beyond the text. Workshopping teachers appropriate shared and close reading structures and strategies for teaching students to read *against* text. For example, we use shared reading strategies such as inferring, questioning, visualizing, predicting, connecting, summarizing, and analyzing to examine issues of power, normativity, and representation in the text, as well as from our meaning-making processes with text. When conducting a literary close reading *against* text, students not only note the author's use of technique, but also critically interrogate how and why certain techniques are used, considering the author's purpose and power in shaping readers' perceptions of normalcy.

When conducting a language close reading *against* text, workshopping teachers not only encourage students to unravel an author's techniques and conventions but also guide them to understand that language and texts are biased. There is power in language, and workshopping teachers deconstruct an author's language decisions to expose how language can be used to manipulate readers.

5

Seeing Text Critically

[R]ight when you think you "get it," you see something else. You can find a million hidden meanings.

—Erika L. Sánchez, *I Am Not Your Perfect Mexican Daughter*

As readers, we always want to "see something else." In search of meaning, workshopping teachers introduce literary theories (e.g., reader response, New Criticism, rhetorical, moral/philosophical, historical/biographical, New Historicism, poststructuralism, archetypal, psychoanalytic, Marxist, feminist, queer, critical race, critical disability, etc.) and encourage students to view texts through various historical, cultural, and political lenses, interrogating text and questioning ideologies that construct the social realities in which we participate.

Never has the study of theory been more important. If we want to foster greater understanding of difference, then we need to provide students with opportunities to inhabit diverse theoretical frameworks and see through multiple perspectives. Chapter 5 shares why and how to teach multiple theories when workshopping for democracy and justice. When we adopt different theoretical approaches, we broaden our critical consciousness and expand the ways in which we might see and understand, perhaps discovering a "million hidden meanings."

Why Teach Theory?

Some might consider the study and application of literary criticism to be esoteric. In a world where students have to practice hard lockdowns and wear masks, how is theory relevant? When we teach students to read texts through a variety of theoretical lenses, we are helping them to interpret the word and the world through multiple perspectives. We are helping them to see how different people can view and interpret texts and events differently. We are helping them to better understand the mindsets of others and the possible origins of viewpoints. We are providing them with the tools not only to make sense of text but also to make sense of one another and the world. Never has literary theory been more important to teach.

Teachers who workshop for democracy and justice view texts through various lenses. No single vision dominates teaching. Not New Criticism, with our close reading of the author's techniques or intentions. Not historical/biographical criticism, with our exploration of the times and life of the work and author. Not reader response, with our prompting and sharing of personal experiences related to the text. Workshopping teachers apply varied theoretical approaches to various genres to broaden students' critical awareness and expand the ways in which we might see and understand.

When we workshop for democracy and justice, a primary aim is to broaden the ideological scope of critical thinking, so we adopt several critical stances. While we would certainly view Orwell's *Animal Farm* through a Marxist or historical/biographical lens, we might also view the text through feminist and moral/philosophical lenses. Similar to stretching, we improve our mental flexibility when we inhabit different theoretical perspectives. Reading through multiple critical lenses gives us the ability to recognize complexity in texts and in the world. As Carpenter (2000) maintains, "perhaps it will do us some good to get inside another way of thinking, even if just for a short span of time" (p. 4).

Studying theory helps us discover elements of our own ideology as well as recognize the ideology of others. After all, critical approaches are already evident in our teaching practice. Do you introduce a text by providing background about the life and times of the author and work (historical/biographical)? As you are reading, do you ask students what they like or dislike about certain characters or their actions (reader response)? Do you engage students in deep discussions about what they can learn from their reading, the themes and morals of the text (moral/philosophical)? Different critical perspectives produce different approaches to text, generate very different questions, and lead readers to varying truths.

Teaching theory is necessary for democracy because it ultimately enables us to question power. No authority can impose truth on someone who understands the variance of truths proposed by different ideologies. Studying theory "means no authority can impose a truth on you in a dogmatic way—and if some authority does try, you can challenge that truth in a powerful way, by asking what ideology it is based on" (Bonnycastle, 1996, p. 34). Workshopping teachers practice theoretical pluralism so that students can see multiple perspectives, recognize various ideologies, acknowledge multiple truths, and question despotic authority.

What We Know about Theories

Schools of literary criticism impact how we read and teach text, and students need a framework for comprehending critical study. Following is a brief synopsis of various theories that elaborate how readers respond, how literature works, and how authors write. Please note this is not a comprehensive list. It is a brief review of critical approaches most recognizable in high school English classrooms at this time.

Reader response, introduced in Chapter 3, centers on readers' experiences and meaning-making as they read a text. A few general principles distinguish the theory of reader response. First, reading is believed to be a dynamic, active, and situated process. Meaning is variable and changes with each reader. Meaning happens through an equal exchange between the reader and a text, through a sort of "dialogue" between the reader and the text (Rosenblatt, 1994). Readers arrive at meaning through associative and personal responses, and these responses are shaped by the cultural and social contexts of individual readers. To foster reader response when reading Wes Moore's *The Other Wes Moore: One Name, Two Fates*, Katie asked students, "Can you describe a series of events in your life in which things could have gone drastically different, either in a positive or a negative way?"

New Criticism is a formalist movement in literary theory in which meaning and power reside within the text. Readers identify specific literary qualities through close reading and pay careful attention to the form and language of the text itself, seeking meaning within the author's techniques or intentions. New Criticism is the prevailing literary theory underlying the current Common Core State Standards for English Language Arts, which exclude other theories. When reading Erika L. Sánchez's *I Am Not Your Perfect Mexican Daughter*, Mary practiced New Criticism as she asked students, "What is the author's purpose in having Julia as a first-person narrator?"

Rhetorical criticism was developed in response to formalism. This school of literary criticism argues that a work cannot be separated from its author, and meaning resides in the author's art of persuasion. Rhetorical critics analyze the symbolic artifacts of discourse and reveal how they work to persuade readers. When reading George Orwell's *Animal Farm*, Cal practiced rhetorical criticism when he had students consider the following quotation, "All animals are equal, but some animals are more equal than others," and then answer the following question: "What is Orwell trying to convince us of, and how is he doing this?"

For **moral/philosophical** critics, literature is the vehicle for contemplating more serious intellectual and moral matters. Texts are selected on the basis of their ennobling qualities and are evaluated holistically for their ethical content. Moral/philosophical critics acknowledge the positive and the negative effects literature can have on readers and therefore use literature to help students understand Socrates's conception of the "good life." To engage students in moral/philosophical criticism when reading *Antigone*, Katie asked: "Who is the most moral character? The least? And why?"

Historical/biographical criticism focuses on the life and times of the author and work. Biographical critics investigate the life of an author, searching primary documents for experiences, thoughts, and feelings that might be associated with the creation of a text. Historical critics also interpret text through a deeper understanding of the time and culture in which the literary work was written. When reading Arthur Miller's *The Crucible*, Liz asked students: " How might the rise of European fascism, anti-Semitism, and the House Un-American Activities Committee have affected the writing of this play?"

When viewing text through a historical lens, it is especially important for teachers workshopping for democracy and justice to ensure that nondominant counterhistories are considered with literary works, especially those that perpetuate deficit ideologies. For example, if teaching Harper Lee's *To Kill a Mockingbird* or Mark Twain's *Adventures of Huckleberry Finn*, our students need to question the textual history represented and search for alternate histories as a means of subverting the beliefs and values perpetuated by the text. For example, Joshua asked his students: "What version of history does this book tell, and what are other versions?"

New Historicism critics also see text through a historical lens, both past and current. A New Historicist examines how the writer's times affected the work, as well as how the current times affect our reading of the work. New Historicists interpret texts as a product of the author's and our times and cultures. When reading Aldous Huxley's *Brave New World*, I asked students: "How do you think your understanding of cloning, Soma, and birth control differs from that of someone who read this novel when it was first published in 1932?"

Poststructuralism maintains that frameworks and systems are social constructs that cannot be trusted to provide order or relay meaning. Because frameworks and systems are fictitious and unstable, there can be no unified truth, only many truths. Poststructural critics do not trust a system such as language to assert truth, so there can be no correct reading of a text. A poststructural critic creates a multifaceted interpretation of a text, analyzing how a text's meanings shift in relation to many variables, usually involving the identities of the reader. Poststructuralism is also concerned with power, its relationship to language, and how these contribute to and/or maintain hierarchy, as well as the ways and places where systems, frameworks, definitions, and certainties break down. To foster a poststructural theoretical approach, a teacher could ask: "Is Steve a trustworthy narrator in Walter Dean Myers's *Monster*? Why or why not?"

Archetypal criticism examines recurring motifs and patterns in literature that represent universal situations and experiences. The archetypal critic assumes that human beings across histories and cultures have had similar experiences and finds meaning in common, recurring symbols, characters, themes, and narrative designs. Common archetypal characters include the child, the hero, the outcast, the temptress, the villain, the star-crossed lovers, the great mother, the wise old man, and the trickster or fox. Archetypal symbols comprise images such as water, sun, colors, shapes, animals, and numbers. Narrative patterns encompass the hero's journey, creation story, loss of innocence, or descent to the underworld. To foster literary criticism as students watched *Pleasantville,* Amy asked: "What archetypes do you notice?"

Psychoanalytic literary criticism builds on Freud's theories of psychology. Freudian concepts include the levels of consciousness, the psyche (i.e., id, ego, superego), defense mechanisms, complexes (e.g., Oedipus, Electra), and dream interpretation. Freudian critics recognize literature and a reader's response to literature as a means of expressing the unconscious. We gain insight into the psychology of the author, the text, and ourselves, discovering latent desires, fears, and fantasies when we see a work through a psychoanalytic lens. Mark applied the psychoanalytic lens when he asked: "In what ways is Will influenced by the id, ego, and superego in Jason Reynolds's *Long Way Down*?"

Contemporary literary theories are especially relevant for teachers workshopping toward democracy and justice. Contemporary theories relate to issues of identity categories, including class, gender, sexuality, and race. Marxism, feminism, queer, critical race, and critical disability theories also guide readers to interrogate text features with considerations of power and oppression, inviting us to "consider the kinds of prevailing ideologies that helped construct the social realities in which we participate (or sometimes become unwitting participants)" (Appleman, 2015, p. 58).

While contemporary literary theories are especially relevant for better understanding the word and the world, their use can be challenged in the classroom. Those who hold power may resist ideas that disrupt the status quo or expose societal inequities. Workshopping teachers understand multiple perspectives and teach multiple theories. We do not mandate or impose one way of seeing or understanding. Instead, we offer choices and empower students with a variety of literary filters through which to see and understand text, selves, one another, and the world.

Marxism considers the political content as well as the historical, cultural, and political context of a work, author, and reader. Marxist theory explores the ways in which texts and readers are socially constructed and views text through the author's and the reader's prevailing ideologies, their political and historical contexts. When we see through a political lens, we notice the social structures portrayed in a particular work and analyze how power is allocated among different social groups. Marxist literary theory brings greater visibility to issues of privilege, class, money, ideology, and resistance that are embedded in texts (and readers) and helps us interpret literature around issues of justice—whether or not a work supports or challenges typical power relationships. To prompt a Marxist reading of Lorraine Hansberry's *A Raisin in the Sun*, Alex asked: "How does each character value money, class, and power differently in this play? How does your own understanding of the relationships between money, class, privilege, and power affect your reading of this play?"

Feminist criticism examines text for its patriarchal ideology and considers the marginalization of women as readers and writers. Critics contemplate the gender of the author, its relevance to how the text is written and received; the gender of characters, how they reflect or confront prevailing ideologies of how men and women are situated; and the gender of readers, the ways in which interpretations are constructed (Appleman, 2015). Feminist critics explore how a text, author, reader, or reading supports or challenges the economic, political, social, and psychological oppression of women. When reading *Hamlet*, Ashley asked: "How are the relationships between Hamlet and Ophelia and Ophelia and Polonius portrayed?"

Teachers workshopping for democracy and justice problematize stereotypical understandings of gender with students when applying a feminist lens. There can be many constructions of femininity and masculinity, so when we apply a feminist lens, we want to reach beyond a dualistic approach. Workshopping teachers engage students in discussions around gender differences, including the following: What does difference mean? How might we read difference? Does it matter? Whose interests are best served by such a dualistic polarization? Are we able to write differently, to read differently, to construct other stories than these intensely polarized forms? And what conditions make that possible? We also need to address the multiplicity, differences, and nuances within the category of "woman" and consider the intersections of race, religion, and culture with gender (Gilbert, 1997).

Queer theory, influenced by feminist and poststructuralist criticism, explores and challenges binary labels such as homosexual/heterosexual, man/

woman, and masculine/feminine. Critics are interested in the breakdown of these binaries, recognizing definitions, constructions, and biologies of "male" and "female" as in a state of flux. Theorists problematize assumptions about sexuality as well as the linguistic constructs designed to maintain the current power structure, investigating the construction, production, and maintenance of what is considered "normal" in order to challenge the status quo. Queer theory provides a critical lens with which to disrupt traditional power hierarchies and imagine alternate ways of being in the world. As with other contemporary theories, queer theory can be used to revitalize classics. When reading Harper Lee's *To Kill a Mockingbird*, Nicole asks: "What kind of support (if any) is given Scout, who questions the masculine/feminine binary? What happens to her as a result?"

Critical race theory examines race and racism across dominant modes of expression. Critical race theorists acknowledge society as racialized and whiteness as normative and therefore seek to expose and challenge practices that enable racism. To counter prejudice, theorists explore how victims of systemic racism are affected by cultural perceptions of race, examining sociocultural forces that shape how we perceive, experience, and respond to racism, including how race interacts with other identities such as gender, class, and sexual orientation. Critical race theory is an important intellectual and social tool for the "deconstruction of oppressive structures and discourses, reconstruction of human agency, and construction of equitable and socially just relations of power" (Ladson-Billings, 1998, p. 9). To foster a critical race lens, teachers can explore how race and racism manifest in literature. When reading Isabel Quintero's *Gabi, a Girl in Pieces*, Grace asked students to consider: "How do Gabi's race and gender affect her identity?"

A critical race theoretical lens should be used to challenge subtle (and not so subtle) racist ideologies in canonical texts. Teachers who workshop for democracy and justice can use critical race theory to confront implicit (and explicit) racism and to challenge dominant ideology presented in texts. Macaluso (2017) encourages us to read *To Kill a Mockingbird* through the lens of old and new racism. Old racism highlights more explicit instances of textual racism, whereas new racism exposes more implicit racism—those hidden ideological systems of power and domination gained through privileging whiteness. To help students uncover invisible systems of racism and move beyond the mere identification of race and racism, we might ask: "What unjust systems are evident in this novel? How does this novel reproduce cultural norms or narratives about African Americans (in terms of incarceration, economic disparity, and subordination)?"

Critical disability theory analyzes disability in political, historical, social, aesthetic, ethical, and cultural contexts. This theoretical lens explores images and descriptions of disability, social norms that define attributes as impairments, prejudices against people with disabilities (ableism), and the ways narrative relates to disability (*Introduction to Literary Theory*, n.d.). Disability theorists consider the sociopolitical constructions of disability and the impacts of these constructions on oppressed persons, engaging in critical intersectional analysis that scrutinizes normative ideologies among multiple categories of identity, including race, class, gender, and sexuality. Aware of the relationships between disability and power, theorists direct their work toward activism and attend to devalued persons in support of justice.

English teachers can help students see through a critical disability lens by critically examining texts for their representations of disability and normalcy. For example, when reading Mark Haddon's *The Curious Incident of the Dog in the Night-Time*, we can ask: "How is Christopher's autism presented by the author? How does Christopher deal with his disability? How does this novel support or challenge normative ideologies about disabilities?"

How to Teach Theories

Workshopping teachers make theoretical approaches explicit by naming, explaining, and applying different schools to a variety of texts. As we know, texts transmit ideology, and a growing awareness of theories empowers readers to recognize and analyze ideology not only in text but also in ourselves, each other, and the world.

To first foster awareness of personal ideologies, I begin each school year by introducing students to reader response during our unit focused on Identities and Perspectives. I explain that each reader transacts with a text differently. Each reader brings a personal, cultural, social, economic, and political context to each reading, and as a result, each student's response is unique and valid. Through reader response, we can come to better understand, appreciate, and respect the differences among us.

Next, I guide students to consider the factors shaping their individual responses to text (see Chapter 3). What factors of background and culture (e.g., race, religion, socioeconomic status, language, sexual orientation) are shaping their responses? What do their responses reveal about their beliefs, values, assumptions, and attitudes that derive from certain ideologies? In this way, I am prompting students to search for social and cultural influences. The more we uncover about our own experiences and consider how these shape our understandings, the better we can interpret the experiences and understandings of others.

Teachers who workshop for democracy and justice help to develop students' awareness of multiple responses, experiences, and perspectives, knowing that the best way to recognize and transcend bias is through dialogue with those possessing different ideologies. Reader response heightens our awareness of varied ways of reading, meaning-making, and being. Sharing and acknowledging different beliefs and assumptions, and reflecting and analyzing on their origins, lays an important foundation for critical study.

Along with fostering students' awareness of their responses and prompting critical reflection on these responses, we can also use a variety of texts to increase awareness of diverse perspectives and ideologies that shape viewpoints. For example, Jon Scieszka's *The True Story of the 3 Little Pigs! By A. Wolf* offers readers the big bad wolf's take on the classic tale. John Gardner's *Grendel* is a retelling of *Beowulf* from the mindset of the monster. Lisa Klein's young adult novel *Ophelia* and Tom Stoppard's play *Rosencrantz and Guildenstern Are Dead* offer alternate views of Shakespeare's *Hamlet*.

We can also introduce students to texts with multiple points of view, including Randa Abdel-Fattah's *When Michael Met Mina*, Chimamanda Ngozi Adichie's *Americanah*, Louise Erdrich's *Love Medicine*, Imbolo Mbue's *Behold the Dreamers*, Karen M. McManus's *One of Us Is Lying*, Toni Morrison's *Song of Solomon*, Marieke Nijkamp's *This Is Where It Ends*, Jennifer Niven's *All the Bright Places* and *Holding Up the Universe*, R. J Palacio's *Wonder*, Rainbow Rowell's *Eleanor and Park*, Lisa Williamson's *The Art of Being Normal*, and Nicola Yoon's *The Sun Is Also a Star*. Before embarking on critical study, we want students to consider the beliefs and values shaping their own and others' points of view in order to deconstruct a singular vision and to grasp theoretical pluralism.

Through reading, responding, and writing, students can gain an understanding of and appreciation for other perspectives. As mentioned in Chapter 4, students can rewrite texts, adding or switching a point of view as a means of resisting and restorying a singular and dominant vision. In critical workshopping classrooms, students don't just read multiple texts; they respond and write critically to gain the critical discernment necessary to see through multiple, critical, cultural, political, and theoretical lenses.

To expand their view, students can write in response to questions designed to promote critical thinking. I provide students with a series of questions to select from and respond to in reading blogs. These questions subtly introduce students to the theoretical frameworks that shape our points of view. Workshopping teachers might ask students to consider the following:

- Who does this novel think its readers are? What does it assume about the reader?

- What roles do power, class, gender, and race play in this text?
- What societal structures, or social groups, are evident in this text? Are there class conflicts? Describe.
- How are female characters portrayed? Do these portrayals reinforce or undermine sexual stereotypes?
- How do you think your gendered self affects your reading of this text?
- Are there any characters with disabilities in this text? If so, how are they represented?
- Does this character or text support or challenge normative ideologies about disabilities?
- Do any characters challenge normative ways of thinking about gender?
- How is race presented in this text?

When reading Lee's *To Kill a Mockingbird,* Rollins opted to consider how his gendered self affected his reading of this novel:

> I identify as a man, so I think it is fair to say that I connect more easily with characters like Atticus and sympathize more easily with say, Tom or Boo Radley than perhaps I do with characters like Calpurnia or Helen (if I don't check my bias). That's in the most literal sense, but on a deeper level, I think my identification as male, could make it easier for me to excuse the behavior of characters like Atticus, Bob Ewell, etc. because of the ways in which society has deemed them to be appropriate male characteristics or traits. . . . I wouldn't say I'm particularly "manly" by any stretch of the imagination, but I could see the ways in which men being portrayed as political leaders, pillars of the community, saviors, etc., would be easier for me to accept at face value, as someone who identifies as male, than perhaps other's might who do not.

Whereas Rea considered the interrelationship between race and power:

> *To Kill a Mockingbird* explores the way in which several types of prejudice worm their way into everyday life, particularly how racism is ingrained in the criminal justice system. This particular struggle creates a power imbalance between the white people and the black people in Maycomb. The white people control the status quo and have the final say in the courts of law, and because of racist attitudes, black people accused like Tom Robinson are found guilty of crimes they may have never committed in the first place, incriminated only by the color of their skin.

> Even with characters who do not take the stand in the courtroom, we see an imbalance of power between characters of differing races. The black people of Maycomb live in cabins away from the white people. In addition, the few black names we do receive in the book other than Tom's are those belonging to women who are also servants of the white people, despite the mirage of being "hired help." Calpurnia, Sophie, and Helen are all black women in the book who are given side-roles and act as servants to white characters with more prominent voices.

Once students have a heightened awareness of the ideologies shaping texts and our understanding of them, workshopping teachers introduce and apply literary theories to multiple texts and genres across the school year. All genres warrant critical study, including canonical texts, young adult novels, picture books, nonfiction text (e.g., essays, articles, memoirs, biographies, websites, reviews), graphic novels, short stories, films (including documentaries), poetry, plays, lyrics, art, social media (e.g., TikTok, Instagram, Facebook, YouTube, influencers), and social movements.

The selection of texts and theories depends on a teacher's purpose. Of course, some texts may demand certain theoretical approaches more than others. Kate Chopin's "The Story of an Hour," Charlotte Perkins Gilman's "The Yellow Wallpaper," or Virginia Woolf's *A Room of One's Own* necessitate a feminist lens, for instance. But these same texts might also be viewed through historical/biographical, New Historicism, poststructural, queer, or Marxist lenses. Workshopping teachers teach to expand their students' critical awareness.

For example, in my unit focused on Identities and Perspectives, I show the first eighteen minutes from an episode of the Netflix series *Black Mirror*, titled "Nosedive." This episode offers viewers a biting satire on social media and the role it plays in identity formation as well as gender expectations. After we watch the clip, I divide students into groups of four. After introducing the purpose of literary criticism and providing a very brief overview of the moral/philosophical, feminist, Marxist, and New Historicist perspectives, I assign each group a critical lens through which to view the episode. Students conduct further research online and are given a series of open-ended questions to guide their thinking (see Figure 7). Once students are confident in their collaborative critical analysis of the story, I jigsaw the groups, creating new groups consisting of members from other schools of criticism, allowing students to hear alternative perspectives of the same text. In this way, we are able to hear different interpretations. This same structure can be adapted and applied to a variety of genres. See Figure 8 for the questions Liz and Isis generated to prompt students to think critically about Arthur Miller's *The Crucible*.

Ultimately, our goal as workshopping teachers is to move students from analyzing the page to analyzing the world. Theoretical perspectives provide an ideal opportunity to read the word and the world together as we use theoretical lenses to view society as text. Imagine viewing social movements such as #MeToo through a feminist and queer lens, or #BlackLivesMatter through a critical race and Marxist lens. What about a historical event such as the storming of the

You Be the Critic!

You have just watched a clip from the Netflix series *Black Mirror*, titled "Nosedive." Just as we may "read" a text, we can "read" any form of media. I'd like you to read this episode in light of a particular kind of literary theory. I want you to consider it deeply from a particular theoretical perspective. You will be placed in a group and assigned a particular school of literary criticism. Work together and think deeply. Use the following questions to guide your discussion. Fill a page with your notes and ideas, and be prepared to lead a discussion with the class about your new understanding of the text.

- **Moral/philosophical**: For you, literature is a vehicle for discussion of themes and morals—a text should be studied for its important issues and deep meanings.

  What do you think are morals or values or deep meanings expressed through this episode? What evidence can you provide from the episode to prove this? Who do you think is the most moral character? The least? Why do you think so? Are the writers criticizing a certain moral code?

- **Feminist**: You concern yourself with images of women and the feminine in literature and how women are portrayed and differentiated from men. You intend to raise our consciousness about sexual exploitation and alienation.

  What images of women are projected, and are they different from men? What is the relationship between social media culture and women versus that of men? Are there differences? What does this "difference" mean? What evidence can you provide from the episode to support your beliefs?

- **Marxist**: Your interpretation of literature centers on issues of justice and whether a work supports or challenges typical power relationships. You believe that literature must direct our attention to social matters, not remove us from them.

  What is the role of social class in this episode? Does the episode portray a positive view of the "ruling class"? What is the significance of money to different characters? What evidence can you provide from the episode to support your beliefs?

- **New Historicism**: You look for connections between literature and the general culture, both the one it was written in and the one it is being read in, and the difference between those lenses.

"Nosedive" first aired in 2016. What does this text suggest about today's culture, especially in relation to social media? How do you think your experiences watching this episode differ from that of a viewer 7 years ago? Why do you think this?

FIGURE 7. You Be the Critic jigsaw handout for students.

Feminist:
What role do women play in *The Crucible*?
What role did women in this play have in relation to the men in this play?

Historical/Biographical:
What major historical event was happening during the time this play was written? How does this event shape the play as a whole?
Describe the roles of men, women, and religious leaders during the Puritan era. Have these roles changed?

Moralist:
In your opinion, who is the most and least moral character? How are morals considered throughout this play?

New Historicism:
How are the events in this play similar to the events in our current society?
How is the process in which those who are wrongfully convicted in *The Crucible* similar to how people are wrongfully convicted today?

FIGURE 8. Questions to prompt critical thinking about *The Crucible*.

US Capitol in 2021? How might we view this event through psychoanalytic, Marxist, and critical disability theoretical lenses? Or the COVID-19 pandemic through archetypal, feminist, critical race, and Marxist lenses? Critical synthesis empowers citizen readers with tools to view the world and one another with a greater understanding of varying perspectives and their origins. When we practice reading through theoretical approaches, we broaden our critical consciousness and expand the ways we might see and understand the word, the world, ourselves, and each other.

Chapter Summary

Teachers who workshop for democracy and justice teach students to read text through varied theoretical lenses, helping them to interpret the word and the world through multiple perspectives. Workshopping teachers practice theoretical pluralism so that students can see diverse viewpoints, recognize various ideologies, acknowledge multiple truths, and question despotic authority. Workshopping teachers make theoretical approaches (e.g., reader response, New Criticism, rhetorical, moral/philosophical, historical/biographical, New Historicism, poststructuralism, archetypal, psychoanalytic, Marxist, feminist, queer, critical race, critical disability, etc.) explicit by naming, explaining, and applying different schools to myriad texts.

To prepare students for critical study and grow their awareness of different ideologies, workshopping teachers engage students in reader response and critical reflection on these responses. Teachers use reading, writing, and questioning to broaden students' understanding of points of view and to introduce theoretical frameworks that shape points of view. A growing awareness of theories empowers readers to recognize and analyze ideology not only in text but also in ourselves, each other, and the world.

6

Talking Back and Beyond

What's the point of having a voice if you're gonna be silent in those moments you shouldn't be?

—Angie Thomas, *The Hate U Give*

Workshopping teachers encourage students to use their voices. We know talk enhances our understanding of text, but it also helps us better understand ourselves, others, and the world. Chapter 6 reviews workshop structures that encourage talk and reflection on talk when workshopping the canon for democracy and justice.

Workshopping teachers provide opportunities for students to talk about texts, hear various viewpoints, and reflect on talk through Socratic circles and book clubs. During Socratic circles, students practice democratic discourse and contemplate different opinions and points of view that sometimes challenge their own beliefs. In book clubs, students participate in conversations around young adult texts to foster understanding of different life experiences and worldviews. Students engage in critical conversations, speaking back to texts and reflecting intermittently on their language use during and after Socratic circles and book clubs. Through these workshop structures, students develop their voices and learn not to be silent.

Why Talk?

Historically speaking, teachers have always talked too much. More than a century ago, Stevens (1912) found teachers talking 64 percent of the time during classroom discussions; Bellack et al. (1966) found teachers talking three times more than students in the 1960s; Barnes (1992) found teachers doing the majority of the talking in the 1970s; and Goodlad (1984) found discussion accounted for only 5.1 percent of class time in the 1980s. Even in the 1990s, discussion took place less than fifty seconds per class in grade 8 and less than fifteen seconds in grade 9 classrooms (Nystrand, 1997). The century may have changed, but Nystrand et al. (2003) still found discussion in only 6.69 percent of 1,151 instructional episodes in grades 8 and 9.

We want to hear dialogue, not monologue, in the workshopping classroom. A discussion is not a lecture led by the teacher; it is instead a sharing of ideas between participants in an interpretive community. Gilles (2010) made clear the connection between critical thinking and talk: "If we want students to do more critical thinking, to probe deeper into texts, and to build ideas with others, then we must rely on talk" (p. 11). Talk promotes ideas. As one student revealed, "I enjoy talking about what I read in class because it gives you everybody's perspective on many different things, which helps you understand these people, understand the literature, and create your own perspective" (Styslinger & Pollock, 2010).

Talk prompted by text is invaluable to students' civic education as they hear and honor different opinions and perspectives. The habits of democracy, Dewey reminds us, include the ability to "grasp the point of view of another" (cited in Moyers, 1992). We need to build intellectual communities through discourse in the workshopping classroom and guide students to conduct themselves through an exchange of ideas; listen appreciatively to the ideas of others; frame their own thoughts with evidence and examples; speculate and hypothesize, evaluate and analyze; and show how they can extend their thinking and the thinking of others (Beers & Probst, 2013). When teachers encourage student voices, we are helping to prepare an engaged citizenry.

To encourage student voices, we foster a classroom culture that embraces questions and inquiry and empowers students to take informed and active stances about larger issues in the world. We engage students in dialogue as a means of developing social and critical consciousness. Students speak back to texts, questioning the world, their beliefs, and the beliefs of others. Through engagement in workshop structures and strategies, students learn to listen and disagree respectfully and to recognize the power of group conversation where democratic conditions exist and authentic exchanges can occur around issues of moral, social, and cultural significance.

What We Know about Socratic Circles

Socrates was convinced that the surest way to attain reliable knowledge was through the practice of disciplined conversation, which he called a "dialectic." A dialectic is the art or practice of examining opinions or ideas logically, often by the method of question and answer, so as to determine their validity. A Socratic circle creates a dialectic in which participants seek deeper understanding of complex ideas through rigorously thoughtful dialogue.

Before participating in a Socratic circle, students read and take notes on an assigned text. Articles related to a critical unit focus and essential questions can be found on commonlit.org or newsela.com. I also like to scour Kelly Gallagher's Article of the Week archives for relevant texts (kellygallagher.org). Students create questions to ask one another about what they have read. They are then divided into an inner and an outer circle. The inner circle engages in a question-based discussion while students in the outer circle listen carefully to the inner circle, providing feedback once their discussion of the text is complete. Then the circles exchange roles and positions (Copeland, 2005).

While a Socratic circle can focus on one or more specific text, it can also support inquiry into a more general unit focus or essential questions, encouraging students to cite examples and evidence from a variety of genres. For example, students can explore the relationship between identities, perspectives, and power (see Appendix A) and draw on a variety of texts read throughout the unit. Teachers workshopping for democracy and justice use Socratic circles to promote discussions that foster new ways of looking at the world, prompted by units and questions.

Teachers prepare students for circle participation with how-to mini-lessons. A how-to mini-lesson explains how to do something. I have found it helpful to, as a class, watch a Socratic circle on YouTube or TeacherTube and ask students to take notes on what they see and hear (see Figure 9). Following a large-group discussion, we establish procedures for Socratic circles and guidelines for class participation. I also provide a how-to mini-lesson on questioning. Socratic circles open with a question, and a good opening question leads students to speculate, evaluate, define, and clarify ideas prompted by their critical reading. Responses to the opening question generate new questions, leading to new responses.

A Socratic circle encourages voice. It provides students with an opportunity to talk back to and beyond text without the strict control of right answers. Students have a conversation, gain various perspectives, and try on various opinions and viewpoints. As students contemplate different points of view, they become more aware of diverse opinions, ideas, and ideologies. Socratic

What Do I See?	What Do I Hear?
	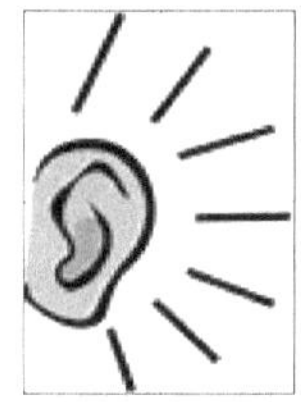

FIGURE 9. Student handout for recording notes when watching a Socratic circle or book club.

circles facilitate the growth and development of responsible citizens as students practice democratic discourse and prepare for public dialogue.

How to Foster Democracy and Justice with Socratic Circles

What to Read

Workshopping teachers think critically about the texts used to prompt discussion for Socratic circles. We want to foster talk that focuses on contentious, real-world issues related to the unit focus and essential questions. To foster a greater understanding of multiple perspectives, I like to provide students with a minimum of two texts, often sourced from different news networks, to read prior to participation. These two texts may offer contrasting viewpoints on a common topic. This juxtapositioning (McLaughlin & De Voogd, 2004) encourages student readers to investigate bias and critically analyze how authors craft events from different points of view. When we provide students with multiple news coverage of a common topic, we simultaneously increase understanding of diverse experiences, beliefs, and values while heightening their critical consciousness of the power structures shaping points of view.

The widest disseminators of news, commentary, and ideas in the United States are entrenched among a small number of the world's wealthiest corporations (Bagdikian, 2004). At the time this book was drafted, five corporations own most of the US media outlets. Currently, the biggest media conglomerates in America are AT&T, Comcast, Disney, CBS, and Fox Corporation. Follow me down this rabbit hole. CNN is owned by AT&T, which owns WarnerMedia (formerly Time Warner Inc.). Fox News used to be owned by 21st Century Fox, which was bought by Disney in 2019. Preceding this acquisition, 21st Century Fox spun off the Fox Broadcasting Company, Fox television stations, Fox News Channel, Fox Business, FS1, FS2, and Fox Deportes, which became Fox Corporation, which is retained by the Murdoch family. Murdoch owns News Corp and *The New York Post*, HarperCollins, and *The Wall Street Journal*, among other assets. The owner of NBC News, MSNBC, and CNBC is Comcast, whose parent company is NBCUniversal, which also owns Telemundo. ABC News is a branch of Walt Disney Television, which is a branch of Disney Media Networks, which is part of the Walt Disney Company, which owns, well, too much to list here. CBS News is owned by the CBS Corporation, which is owned by National Amusements, which owns Viacom, which owns Paramount Pictures, Comedy Central, MTV, Nickelodeon, BET, CMT, VH1, and Simon & Schuster. The gist of this paragraph is that only a few companies are responsible for deciding what information is shared about the world. Initially, the internet was embraced as a liberating force from corporate media, but over time, online news sites have also become properties of media conglomerates or become digital conglomerates in their own right (e.g., Google/Alphabet, Facebook, Amazon, Apple).

Now that our media critical consciousness is raised, it is vital that we guide students to critically consider what they are reading, who is doing the writing (and with whom they are affiliated), why it is being written, and how it is being written. Before setting students up in a Socratic circle, workshopping teachers purposefully provide texts that offer contradictory viewpoints on a common topic. For example, in their unit focused on Beliefs and Values with Sophocles's *Antigone* as a core text, Katie, Michael, and Josh prompted students to consider their stance on the protests following the death of George Floyd. Before participating in the Socratic circle, students read both "The George Floyd Protests Are a Rebellion against an Unjust System" by Philip V. McHarris, published in *The Guardian,* as well as "Anger Is Justified, Riots Never Are" by

Michael Brendan Dougherty, published in *National Review.* Similarly, Maggie and Franny had students read "Why Protest Events Are Not a Waste of Time" by Tom Head, published online in *ThoughtCo.*, and "Why Street Protests Don't Work" by Moisés Naim, published in *The Atlantic*, for their unit focused on Challenging Authority, George Orwell's *1984*, and Angie Thomas's *The Hate U Give.* Appendix B provides a list of articles that offer different perspectives and sometimes opposing positions from different media outlets or sources that can be used to foster Socratic circles. Workshopping teachers select texts purposefully to raise students' critical consciousness and to help them see texts, one another, and the world through a more critical lens.

How to Question

Once students have read and taken notes on a minimum of two texts broadening points of view, they are ready to engage in Socratic circles and interrogate multiple viewpoints through questioning. Workshopping teachers guide students to ask questions about what a text means, how it comes to mean, and why a text means. Through questioning the text, the author, and each other, we explore the values, beliefs, and ideologies shaping perspectives.

Workshopping teachers guide students to ask critical questions during how-to mini-lessons. Drawing from McLaughlin & De Voogd (2004) and Lewinson et al. (2002), students investigate *what* a text means, asking questions that examine a text's substance, significance, and perspective:

- What issues are raised by the text?
- What does the author want us to think?
- What language and/or visuals are used?
- Whose viewpoint is expressed?
- Are multiple viewpoints expressed?
- Whose perspectives are missing?
- Does this text disrupt commonplace beliefs or attitudes about the topic?
- Does this text encourage you to take action in the world?

Students ponder *who* wrote the text, asking questions that probe an author's motivations and interests shaping their perspective:

- What is the author's occupation, class, ethnicity, politics, education, age, gender, etc.?

- Does the author have anything to gain from writing this text (e.g., conflicts of interest)?
- What organized financial, political, ethnic, or other interests are backing this perspective?

Students ponder *how* a text means, asking questions that analyze how a text is crafted to shape and shift perspective:

- How can I tell that a certain viewpoint is expressed?
- How are language and/or visuals used to manipulate readers?
- How might alternative perspectives be represented?

And students consider *why* a text means, asking questions that explore why an author might choose to share a particular perspective on a topic:

- Why do you think the author wants us to think this?
- Why are certain perspectives missing from the text?
- Why do you think the author uses this language and/or visuals?
- Why do you think the author wants to disrupt commonplace beliefs or attitudes about the topic?
- Why do you think the author wants you to take action in the world?

Asking these kinds of questions encourages a critical questioning stance toward text and the world. To encourage multiple viewpoints, students are encouraged to ask questions and seek alternate points of view:

- Who has a different perspective?
- What is another point of view you could take?
- Who has not yet had a chance to speak?

Once students are prepared to ask critical questions, I divide them into an inner and an outer circle. Students participate in two circles, one focused around each text so that they hear diverse perspectives on a similar topic. The inner circle engages in a discussion of the first text while students in the outer circle silently observe the inner circle, providing feedback to the inner circle once their discussion of the text is complete. The workshopping teacher keeps the discussion of the inner circle focused and moving, directs the feedback of the outer circle, and assesses and evaluates individual student and group participation. Students then switch inner and outer circle positions and discuss the second text. If more time is available, students can engage in both inner and outer circle positions for each text.

How to Reflect on Talk

Teachers workshopping for democracy and justice think critically about the roles of inside and outside circles. While participants in the inner circle are engaged in reading and speaking positions, participants in the outside circle stand "outside" reading and speaking positions and therefore can help students reflect critically on stances they are taking toward the text, one another, and the world.

Through questioning, an outer circle can help students reflect on their growing critical dispositions (Lewison et al., 2008). It is often difficult for a solitary reader to interrogate their own interpretive frameworks, but an outer circle of peers provides a sort of reflective distance and can prompt those in the inner circle to consider their conscious engagement, their efforts to try on alternative ways of being, and their responsibility to inquiry and reflexivity. A student in the outer circle, for instance, can guide students in the inner circle to practice conscious engagement by asking questions about their use of language, probing how they responded and to whom, prompting critical reflection on the dialogic process. Or the outer circle can nudge those in the inner circle to consider their efforts to try on alternate ways of being, asking if anyone in the inner circle tried on a new stance on the topic to better understand someone else's perspective or experience. Or the outer circle can encourage the inner circle to reflect on their responsibility to inquiry, asking if they questioned, interrogated, and investigated text from a critical stance? Or to ponder their reflexivity, asking if they are aware of any complicity in maintaining the status quo or perpetuating systems of injustice.

During Socratic circles, workshopping teachers use the outer circle to heighten consciousness and foster reflection on critical dispositions. In doing so, participants in the outer circle help participants in the inner circle reflect critically on stances they are taking and foster a greater awareness of diverse perspectives, a necessary attribute for living within a democracy.

What We Know about Book Clubs

Book clubs provide an ideal setting for students to talk about young adult novels, picture books, short stories, informational/explanatory text, graphic novels, poetry, lyrics, images, social media—any text used to expand a unit focus and explore essential questions. Book clubs are made up of small groups of three to five readers who meet on a regular basis, engage in systematic discussions about texts of the members' choice, and use a variety of open-ended response methods to prompt discussion. Membership in a book club varies and can involve the presence of a teacher or volunteer. Topics for discussion come from students, are prompted by a response or mini-lesson, and aim for open and natural conversations around reading and thinking (O'Donnell-Allen, 2006).

Workshopping teachers prepare students for participation in book clubs just as they do for Socratic circles, with how-to mini-lessons. Before beginning book clubs, students observe and then model appropriate, small-group dialogue. They may watch a book club in action, noting what they see and hear (see Figure 9). There are plenty of book club clips available on YouTube or TeacherTube. After students have recorded their observations, they discuss what they saw, focusing on body language, and what they heard, concentrating on appropriate language. As a class, we use these notes to develop a framework for small-group discussion and create a positive list of expectations, which can evolve into a rubric later used for self-evaluation as well as teacher observation.

After students have watched a book club in action, it's time to practice one. I recommend practicing talk with shorter texts such as articles, stories, lyrics, poetry, images, or picture books via a read-aloud. Appendix A offers an array of different genres teachers can draw from. For a book club rehearsal, set up a fishbowl in which three to five volunteer students model a discussion while the rest of the class takes notes or, even better, uses Twitter, Backchannel Chat, or Parlay to share positive examples of oral language, body language, eye contact, and active listening. As a class, share evidence and observations. In this way, we are helping students learn how to talk effectively with one another in small groups.

While we want to establish talk within a clear set of parameters, we also need to be sensitive to the many different ways of talking, which can be affected by culture, by experience with school ways of talking, as well as by access to opportunities to practice ways of talking (Gallas et al., 1996). Discourse is complex and is situated socially, culturally, and historically. We want to create classrooms that acknowledge and embrace many ways of talk.

Throughout the unit, book clubs meet on a regular, predictable schedule, preferably twice a week for twenty-five minutes, to discuss their reading. At the first meeting, groups establish their reading calendar for the unit, ensuring they complete the text by an assigned date. During remaining meetings, they use written notes to guide discussions. A teacher serves as a facilitator but not a group member. Evaluation is by teacher observation as well as student self-evaluation, but if warranted, teachers can still assess reading through more traditional means, including quizzes. Book clubs are capable of being rendered online via Zoom, Microsoft Teams, Google Meet, Blackboard Collaborate Ultra, or another online meeting platform.

Book clubs are necessary workshop structures when teaching for democracy and justice. Freire (2014) strongly encourages dialogue during and after reading, and through book club conversations, students can listen to and learn from the experiences and perspectives of others and, perhaps, reconsider their beliefs about topics prompted by the reading and discussion. Through dialogue, our understandings about readings, one another, and the world are more likely to be challenged, reconsidered, and deepened (Blau, 2003; Hynds & Appleman, 1997). Workshopping teachers promote democracy and justice as we critically engage in reading, questioning, and reflecting during book clubs.

How to Promote Democracy and Justice with Book Clubs

What to Read

If teaching a canonical text, workshopping teachers select young adult texts for students to choose from that provide multiple viewpoints and an array of representations gathered around a unit focus. We can teach canonical and contemporary literature side by side, interrogating voices across texts, unpacking similarities and differences across narratives, and considering these in light of current experiences and realities.

Workshopping teachers are strategic in their choice of supplementary texts, explicitly seeking out genres that represent both students' own groups as well as groups students are less familiar with. As students select contemporary literature, they have the opportunity to read texts more culturally congruent with their own understandings of the world. More culturally responsive texts can allow readers to see themselves and their circumstances reflected in the reading. Such texts may encourage students to explore ways of dealing with day-to-day issues and problems, examine political and social issues, or gain cultural insight and knowledge (Fredricks, 2012). Workshopping teachers purposely select texts that offer mirrors in which students might see their lives and experiences reflected in the lives and experiences of the characters (Bishop, 1990).

Teachers workshopping for democracy and justice also purposely select book club texts that offer windows through which students might view less familiar worlds (Bishop, 1990), encouraging them to engage with the experiences and perspectives of others through contemporary texts. Teachers make deliberate choices of supplementary texts that grow students' multicultural understandings regarding race, ethnicity, gender, sexual orientation, ability, economic situation, religion, and more.

When Dallas and Jillian planned their unit focused on the American Dream and F. Scott Fitzgerald's *The Great Gatsby*, students could choose between the following book club novels: Ibi Zoboi's *American Street*, Angie Thomas's *The Hate U Give*, Jeannette Walls's *The Glass Castle*, Sara Benincasa's *Great*, Zora Neale Hurston's *Their Eyes Were Watching God*, and Erika L. Sánchez's *I Am Not Your Perfect Mexican Daughter*. When Hannah and Ashley planned for a similar unit, they added An Na's *A Step from Heaven*, Sherman Alexie's *The Absolutely True Diary of a Part-Time Indian*, Jason Reynolds and Brendan Kiely's *All American Boys*, and Nicola Yoon's *The Sun Is Also a Star*. In their unit focused on Challenging Authority and George Orwell's *1984*, Franny and Maggie had students select between the following: Malala Yousafzai's *I Am Malala*, Melba Pattillo Beals's *Warriors Don't Cry*, Cory Doctorow's *Little Brother*, Nic Stone's *Dear Martin*, and Jason Reynolds and Brendan Kiely's *All American Boys*. Some books offer students mirrors while others offer windows.

To increase awareness of different cultures, experiences, and perspectives, workshop teachers can jigsaw book clubs. After students have finished reading and discussing their original selections, new book clubs can gather, comprising students who have read different texts. These new groups can discuss the critical essential questions from diverse viewpoints, share summaries of texts they have read, offer experiences of characters, and make comparisons across narratives. Juxtaposing texts through engagement in book clubs can broaden our personal, literary, social, and world perspectives.

How to Question

Workshopping teachers are committed to book clubs that engage students in the difficult conversations books can open for us about the lives of characters in texts and the ways these lives reflect varied experiences in the world. We invite students to inquire, interrogate, and challenge inequities and injustices through text and recognize book clubs as a means of preparing students to live in an increasingly diverse society. Through book club discussions, students can analyze issues of power, privilege, and injustice and gain a deeper understanding of themselves, others, and realities.

Conversations around texts can be a catalyst for change if democratic conditions exist. As a scaffold for student talk, Nachowitz and Brumer (2014) offer a list of sentence starters that lead students to expand, justify, and challenge ideas:

- I want to talk about . . .
- I noticed . . .
- I don't understand . . .
- I wonder why . . .
- I have a different idea . . .
- What in the text makes you believe that?
- I agree with you because . . .
- This reminds me of . . .
- At first I thought ______________; now I think . . .
- Maybe this book is about . . .

While these conversation prompts are helpful for book club conversations, we want to increasingly scaffold students to ask questions that prompt reexamination of their taken-for-granted worldviews. During how-to mini-lessons, workshop teachers encourage students to ask questions that foster cultural understanding. We demonstrate queries that explore how texts can be both mirrors and doors, depending on life experiences:

- Is this book familiar to you in any way?
- Are any characters, settings, situations, language, or ideas in the text similar to what you have experienced?
- How is this book unfamiliar for you?
- In what ways are characters, settings, situations, language, or ideas different from what you have experienced?
- How does this book challenge or change your understanding of people, places, language, or ideas?

We want students to ask those sometimes difficult questions that will expand their worldviews:

- What do you think the author wants you to think about? Why?
- Have you thought about this idea before?
- Does the author provide a different perspective on this idea from your own?
- Does this book disrupt your beliefs or attitudes about the topic? Why?

- In what ways does reading this book increase your understanding regarding race, ethnicity, gender, sexual orientation, ability, economic situation, or religion?

We want students to analyze issues of power, privilege, and injustice:

- Who holds power in this text? Who is privileged in this text?
- Does anyone suffer from inequities or injustices in this text?
- Why do you think the author shows power, privilege, inequities, and injustice in these ways?

And we want students to consider taking action based on what they have read and discussed in book clubs:

- Does this book encourage you to take action in the world?
- If so, why and how?

Similar to participating in Socratic circles, students are also encouraged to use questions to lead others to talk during book club meetings:

- Who has a different experience to share?
- Whose voice has not been heard?
- Could you say more about that?

Workshopping teachers use questioning during book clubs to foster cultural understanding; broaden students' worldviews; analyze issues of power, privilege, and injustice; and promote social agency.

How to Reflect on Talk

Teachers want to foster productive and critical book club conversations, inclusive of all voices and perspectives. To do so, we have to create a democratic classroom environment in which students listen and respond to one another with respect for diverse experiences, ideas, and opinions. "The ways we speak and are spoken to help shape us into the people we become," Shor (1999, p. 1) reminds us, and if we want students to become active and engaged citizens mindful of issues of justice, equity, diversity, and inclusion, then we need to provide opportunities for reflection on talk during and after book club conversations.

Students practice their democratic participation during book clubs. In these small language communities, students make group decisions about reading, speaking, and listening. Together, students talk through conflicts about reading (and not reading), speaking (and not speaking or speaking too much), and listening (and not listening). Talk is necessary for democracy, and increasing our skill at talk could nurture a better democracy (Bomer & Bomer, 2001). Burbules and Rice (1991) list the following as communication virtues that workshop teachers might introduce during how-to mini-lessons: tolerance, patience, self-restraint, disposition for honesty, respect for differences, willingness to listen, the inclination to admit mistakes, and the translation of one's concerns. I use these as a basis for reflection on talk during and after participation in book clubs.

Students can reflect on their participation in book clubs as both speakers and listeners just as they ponder their reader consciousness during critical response (see Chapter 3). During book club conversations, teachers might ask students to pause and consider the following:

- What is the last thing you said? How did you say it? To whom?
- Were your comments honest?
- Were your comments or questions respectful of others? How do you know this?
- What have some of the other book club members said today?
- How did you show that you listened to them?

As we know, evaluation of a book club often includes self-appraisal, and students need to consider both their language and listening skills. Following a book club meeting, teachers might ask students the following:

- Think carefully about your book club conversation today. Write down some things you remember saying during the meeting. What did you say and to whom?
- Look over what you said. Why did you say what you did to this person? What factors might have influenced what you said (e.g., past experience, your family, beliefs, race, ethnicity, gender, religion, ability, sexual orientation, or status)?
- Now consider what your language says about you. Does your language show you to be a reader who is willing to participate and respect the experiences, ideas, and opinions of others? Or does your language show you to be a reader who wants to control the conversation, perhaps by

interrupting others? Or does your language show you to be a reader who is resistant, apathetic, or oppositional? Explain.

- What kind of reader, speaker, and listener do you want to be? Does this match up with the language you used today? Why or why not?
- How will you show yourself as a reader, speaker, and listener at the next book club meeting? Explain.

Reflecting on talk during and following book club meetings encourages students to critically consider their speaking and listening skills, proficiencies necessary for successful participation in a democracy.

Chapter Summary

Talk prompted by text is invaluable to students' civic education as they hear different opinions and perspectives. Workshopping teachers provide opportunities for students to talk about text, hear various viewpoints, and reflect on talk through Socratic circles and book clubs. Workshopping teachers use Socratic circles and book clubs to foster democracy and justice by critically considering what students should read, guiding them to question, and prompting them to reflect.

A Socratic circle creates a dialectic in which participants seek deeper understanding of complex ideas through rigorously thoughtful dialogue. Teachers workshopping for democracy and justice use Socratic circles to promote discussions that focus on real-world issues. We provide students with multiple perspectives on a common topic, simultaneously increasing understanding of diverse experiences, beliefs, and values while heightening critical consciousness of the power structures shaping points of view. Through questioning the text, the author, and one another, we explore the values, beliefs, and ideologies shaping perspectives. During Socratic circles, workshopping teachers use the outer circle to heighten consciousness and foster reflection on critical dispositions.

Book clubs are made up of small groups of readers who meet on a regular basis, engage in systematic discussions about texts of the members' choice, and use a variety of open-ended response methods to prompt discussion. Workshopping teachers are committed to book clubs that allow students the opportunity for critical discourse around culturally responsive texts. We invite students to inquire, interrogate, and challenge inequities and injustices through text and recognize book clubs as a means of preparing students to live in an increasingly diverse society. Workshop teachers use questioning during book clubs to foster cultural understanding; broaden students' worldviews; analyze issues of power, privilege, and injustice; and promote social agency. Reflecting during and following book club meetings encourages students to critically consider their speaking and listening skills, proficiencies necessary for successful participation in a democracy.

7

Writing for Change

I only know that learning to believe in the power of my own words has been the most freeing experience of my life.

—Elizabeth Acevedo, *The Poet X*

In the workshopping classroom, writing emerges naturally from reading and prompts students to make necessary connections between the word and the world. Students write to raise their critical consciousness while reading and in response to a unit focus or essential questions after reading. Chapter 7 introduces structures and strategies for engaging students in both writing-as-process and writing-as-product when workshopping for democracy and justice.

Workshopping teachers support students writing about issues raised in a text and reflected in communities. Students create narrative, informative/explanatory (e.g., list, summary, description, process, definition, comparison-contrast, classification, cause-effect, and problem-solution), argumentative, literary, and multigenre/multimodal papers or projects to demonstrate critical thinking around matters of justice and injustice. Workshopping teachers extend writing from students' lived experiences to center their voices in efforts for reform. Whenever possible, students write for an actual audience, in authentic modes, in ways that amplify their voices across civic contexts. Writing in this way shapes students as critical thinkers and potential activists as they use the power and freedom of their own words to enact change.

What We Know about Writing

According to national guidelines, including the Common Core State Standards (CCSS) and the National Assessment of Educational Progress framework, high school students are expected to engage in writing to persuade (40 percent), writing to explain (40 percent), and writing to convey experience (20 percent). These modes of writing are practiced as students write narrative, informational/explanatory, and argumentative text throughout a focus unit, questioning reading and clarifying meaning. Students also write a culminating narrative, informative/explanatory (e.g., list, summary, description, process, definition, comparison-contrast, classification, cause-effect, problem-solution), argumentative, literary, or multigenre/multimodal paper or project at the conclusion of a unit, demonstrating thinking about a unit focus and/or essential questions. What follows is a brief review of text structures most recognizable in English language arts classrooms.

Narrative tells a real or imagined story. Through the telling of story, we guide others to perceive, know, feel, and experience. As a result of story, we are better able to make sense of the world and of others. To write narrative, students first select a topic worthy of writing about. They then develop the same conventions they so often analyze in other stories, such as setting, characters, plot (i.e., exposition, rising action, climax, falling action, denouement), point of view, dialogue, and theme.

Informative/explanatory text structures include listing and naming, summary/précis, description, process description, definition, comparison-contrast, classification, cause-effect, and problem-solution (Wilhelm et al., 2012). Listing and naming as well as summary/précis are necessary components for creating description, process description, definition, comparison-contrast, classification, cause-effect, and problem-solution. When we **list**, we denote importance. To list, we must name. When we **name**, we confer both meaning and power. We arrange and categorize what we name into lists to connote more and different meaning. Once we have listed and named, we are capable of creating a **summary** or **précis**, which includes key details that are related and shaped to communicate meaning.

Description develops details and enables readers to see, experience, and understand what is described. A student who writes a description fleshes out each detail, demonstrates relationships between details, and even includes some judgment about the details. A description can be organized spatially (e.g., top to bottom or left to right), chronologically, as parts of a whole, or by order of importance. **Process description** outlines in detail the steps or course of an action. Process description allows us to consider, practice, and reflect on a specific activity.

While definitions can be short, an extended **definition** relies on thorough description and deep understanding of a term, concept, or phenomenon. Students can craft extended definitions relevant to the unit focus or in response to essential questions. Students can place the term within a group of ideas to which it most closely belongs, gathering, generating, and analyzing examples and counterexamples (Wilhelm et al., 2012). Students can engage in an authentic research process as they survey and interview others in their efforts to clarify the term.

When we **compare and contrast**, we analyze the similarities and differences of two or more subjects we deem important. Meaning is relayed and an argument made through the analysis of the subjects. A Venn diagram with its overlapping circles can help students visualize what is similar and different. Also helpful, a semantic features analysis prompts students to create a chart, listing the subjects for comparison down the left-hand column while, across the top, listing the features or points of comparison (see Figure 10). Once students have selected points to compare and contrast about their subjects, they develop a thesis or claim (e.g., which is better and why) and decide on an organizational structure. Students can arrange their points in one of three ways: subject by subject, in which all of the points about one subject are combined and followed by all of the points about the second subject; point by point, in which the similarities and differences between each of the points are combined; and likenesses and differences, in which all of the similarities between points are combined and then followed by all of the differences.

Classification helps us see and explain patterns and relationships between ideas. When we classify, we sort a subject into groups or categories to say something meaningful about how a whole relates to a part or a part relates to a whole. We guide students through the process by determining a subject for classification, sorting the subject into useful categories, ensuring the categories fit the same organizing principle, determining a thesis or claim related to the classifications, and providing examples of each category that support the thesis or claim.

Cause-effect text structures are concerned with why something happens (cause), what happens as a result (effect), and the relationship between the reason and the consequence. This structure typically takes one of two forms: it explains how a cause produces specific effects or it explains how specific effects are produced by a cause. Rarely is there a single cause for an effect or

	Setting	Plot	Characters	Dialogue	Theme
Canonical Text					
YA Novel					

FIGURE 10. Semantic feature analysis comparing and contrasting a canonical core text with a YA novel.

a single effect for a cause, so consider the many possibilities. If your causes or effects are previously unknown (and you have discovered either), then you are writing an argument and need a claim, even though the CCSS refer to cause-effect as informational/explanatory text. If a cause or effect is known, then you are writing to inform and need a thesis. Following the claim or thesis, students include a description of the cause, a description of the effect, and an explanation of (or argument for) the cause-effect relationship.

Closely related to cause-effect, **problem-solution** explains the relationship of a problem to a solution or, if the solution or problem is previously unknown, makes an argument for the solution or problem. Students identify a topic; research the problem and solutions; identify the causes of, or solutions to, a problem; write a thesis to inform/explain or claim to argue; and then present their ideas. Students become active problem seekers and solvers through engaging in this inquiry process.

Writing **argument** is mainly about logical appeals and involves claims, evidence, warrants, backing, and rebuttals. Similar to a thesis, a claim needs to be both debatable and defensible. A topic needs to be able to sustain at least two positions, and the claim argues one of these positions. To prove a claim, students gather and organize data; data provide the evidence to substantiate a claim. Students can cite experts, provide facts, offer evidence, list statistics, and state reasons to support the claim. Students can collect data from texts, interviews, surveys, observations, even experiments. Engaging in such a detailed and authentic research process encourages students to understand different points of view. Thus, arguments might begin not just with a claim but with the research process itself. After engaging with the data, students then can state their position and claim with more authority. A warrant explains why the data matter. Data can be used to support a variety of positions, but a warrant clarifies the connection between the claim and the data. A warrant can be stated or assumed. A rebuttal addresses the opposing position. In an argument, we present and refute whatever disputes the claim. We acknowledge and counter different perspectives. Last, the writer presents reasoning or evidence intended to undermine or weaken the claim of an opponent.

Students in the language arts classroom are specifically challenged to construct **literary** arguments, making a defensible yet debatable claim about a work of literature. Students can create analytical arguments about YA novels, picture books, short stories, informational text, graphic novels, social media, poetry, films, television shows, songs, dances, and works of art. Literary arguments can make assertions about characters, themes, plot, literary devices, setting, or craft. As Smith and colleagues (2012) explain, evidence comes from mining a work of literature in support of a claim. The warrant offers a reason for what an author might have intended something to mean or by positing how they might have made different choices if they had wanted to imply a different meaning. The rebuttal considers other perspectives. Foundational to a literary argument is the need for alternative interpretation.

What Is Writing toward Justice?

Workshopping teachers practice a socially oriented approach to the teaching of writing. As students read throughout a unit, we foster critical reflection and write back/in to text, developing our awareness and consciousness. We also encourage writing in a variety of culminating genres, such as those reviewed above, related to everyday justice, power relationships, and other social, cultural, historical, political, or socioeconomical topics relevant to the unit focus and essential questions. Teachers workshopping for democracy and justice support students' meaningful opportunities for socially relevant and conscious writing, guiding students to identify, question, and respond to issues of justice and injustice in text and in life.

All writing is a political act, and when we write toward justice, we raise critical consciousness. We write to foster greater awareness of challenges affecting students, families, and communities. When teachers encourage writing for justice, they center students' experiences and perspectives to promote critical inquiry and writing about matters relevant to their lives (Cammarota & Fine, 2008; Mirra et al., 2015). Students are positioned as active learners and knowledge producers as they explore issues of inequity in the word and in the world. Writing in this way helps shape students as critical thinkers and potential activists.

When students write for social justice, they are ultimately seeking to enact change. Their writing calls for critical reflection and reform. Students may write with a greater sense of purpose because they are not simply writing to meet rubric criteria, but instead are writing to challenge systems of power. When possible, we encourage students to write for an actual audience in ways that "amplify their voices across civic contexts" (Marciano & Warren, 2019, p. 493). Student writing is then read by people whose minds student writers want to change.

Teachers who workshop for democracy and justice appropriate narrative, informational/explanatory, and argumentative text structures. If reading a canonical text, for example, students can write **counternarratives** to subvert the dominant story, share lived experiences, and offset the master narrative. In this way, we are teaching students they have power over words and the power to make new worlds, imagine alternate points of view, and write themselves into a narrative.

Workshopping teachers encourage students to restory and reshape narratives to represent a diversity of perspectives and experiences that are often missing or silenced in mainstream texts (Thomas & Stornaiuolo, 2016). Consider the power a narrator or storyteller holds. Thomas (2018) suggests ways we can encourage students to restory:

- Retell the story in another time and/or place.
- Retell the story from the point of view of a character other than the protagonist, especially a character from a nondominant background and perspective.
- Retell the story in another format. Make it a comic, film a book trailer, turn it into a picture book for younger readers. (What's lost? What's gained? What did you learn?)
- Retell the story by changing the ending or beginning.
- Retell the story by writing what happens next.
- Retell the story by writing yourself, your family, and your friends into the action.

At the conclusion of units, students can also write culminating narratives, crafting new stories in which characters experience persecution, demonstrate agency, or ponder identity.

Students can write informational/explanatory and argumentative texts as they write for change. They can create a **list** of the different perspectives gained by A in David Levithan's *Every Day*, **naming** and **summarizing** each. Students might chronologically **describe** racism after reading Jason Reynolds and Ibram X. Kendi's *Stamped*, or create a **process description** for how to defend civil rights after reading Alex Haley's *Malcolm X*. Likewise, students can craft extended **definitions** for *American* or *identity* in relation to a unit focus. Students can critically **compare and contrast** a core canonical text with a young adult novel, comparing and contrasting such features as the setting, plot, characters, dialogue, and theme of the two works. Students might **classify** in relation to a unit focus (e.g., different kinds of identities or different kinds of American dreams) or in relation to an essential question (e.g., What are different identities we portray? How do we persecute others?).

Certain essential questions can lead to an exploration of **cause-effect** relationships. In a unit centered on Rebellion, students might explore the causes for rebellion. Texts read within a unit may also warrant an exploration of cause-effect relationships: What are the causes and effects of Quinn's initial silence in

Jason Reynolds and Brendan Kiely's *All American Boys*? Other questions and texts lend themselves to the **problem-solution** format: How can we combat racism in our community? What problems does the other Wes Moore face, and how could he surmount them?

And students can write **arguments**. *Some freedoms need to be curtailed in the interests of national security* is a claim written by a student in response to a unit focused on Freedom of Thought, Speech, and Expression. *There are those who believe that the rights listed in the First Amendment must be protected at all costs* is the rebuttal that introduces an alternative view to the initial claim. Students can craft **literary arguments** and make judgments about characters and their actions: *Richard should be charged with two hate crimes in Dashka Slater's* The 57 Bus. Students can write arguments about the central ideas of a text and evaluate those ideas: Monster *offers a social commentary on the treatment of Black youth in America's juvenile justice system.* Or students can write evaluative arguments, offering evidence about the quality of the text itself: *The characters, plot, and theme of* The Absolutely True Diary of a Part-Time Indian *reveal the real-world challenges faced by many teens today.*

How to Challenge Dominant Writing Discourse

In composition studies, the term *modes of discourse* is often used to refer to the categories of written texts. Yet Gee (1989) also writes of Discourse as "a sort of 'identity kit' which comes complete with the appropriate costume and instructions on how to act, talk, and often write, so as to take on a particular role that others will recognize" (p. 7). Let's think about Gee's definition in relation to the more familiar modes of discourse. According to Gee, Discourses possess and wield power because some people have access to them, having previously learned the (unwritten) rules, while others must undergo a sort of apprenticeship to learn the expectations of a Discourse, including how to speak and/or write in a particular mode, for a particular context, for a particular audience. I suggest that the traditional modes of discourse such as those described above are Discourses, because writing in these prescribed forms demands that students "fit in" and learn by "saying-doing-being-valuing-believing" (p. 6). These composition Discourses advantage some and disadvantage others. Teachers workshopping toward democracy and justice can disrupt dominant written Discourse with multigenre and multimodal writing.

Multigenre

In contrast to the more traditional modes of discourse, multigenre text interweaves multiple text structures and threads them together. A multigenre paper or project is not an uninterrupted expository essay, nor a seamless narrative, nor a collection of poems. It is composed of many modes, each piece self-contained, making a point of its own. As Romano (2000) describes, "each genre is a color slide, complete in itself, possessing its own satisfying composition, but also working in concert with the others to create a single literary experience" (p. 4).

A multigenre paper arises from a writer's research, experience, and imagination. The writing might be centered on a unit focus or in response to an essential question, but the multigenre format allows students to respond through a variety of different forms beyond the school-based modes of Discourse. Multigenre writing empowers all students to draw on modes they are familiar with, combining print genres with visual text such as charts, photos, Snaps, cartoons, Bitmojis, Animojis, maps, and the many genre possibilities that technology and social media offer.

In addition to many genres, a multigenre paper might also contain many voices, not just the author's. The multigenre format encourages writers to play with a variety of perspectives. The multiple modes of discourse are then connected by an idea (or focus or question) and sometimes by language, images, and content. Authors create coherence by including an introduction, a table of contents, and a reflection that clarifies for the reader the relationship between the multiple genres.

Multigenre composition challenges dominant written Discourse by offering multiple representations of knowing and by encouraging students to interrogate multiple viewpoints. Rather than providing a singular demonstration of a truth, students are encouraged to explore various truths, a task much better suited for fostering critical thinking within this democratic, diverse society. For example, students can examine a social issue from a variety of perspectives and ensure that multiple voices are represented in the creation. Relying on a single genre limits our ability to communicate multiple meanings. Different genres allow student authors to communicate different kinds of information and include different points of view.

In a unit focused on Gender, my students wrote a culminating multigenre paper that represented their thinking through class readings and conversations. I asked students to answer one of our essential questions: What role does gender play in daily life? I wanted students to embrace writing and research as a personal and freeing experience—as a means of exploring themselves, their values, and their roles in society. Their ways of seeing and saying could appear in multiple forms such as poetry, prose, lists, drama, art, and exposition. They could mix fact with imagery, memory with imagination, in their efforts to convey thinking and knowing to others. Multigenre writing encouraged students to play with a variety of voices, perspectives, and ideas, as evidenced by Felicia, a self-identified female, who wrote:

> I hate girls. They are always trying to play with us boys. Why can't they leave us guys alone? They wear stinky perfume. They have cooties. Girls are always combing and brushing their hair. They are stupid. They always cry about everything. I hate it when they run up and try to kiss you. Gross. They don't know how to play football, and they don't know how to play war. They just don't know how to die right.

Over twenty years ago, Slack (2001) fused social justice with multigenre writing by having students compose multigenre research papers around a movement. Ninth-grade students selected human trafficking, poverty, and beauty images as a basis for their writing. When students are no longer limited by the singleness of voice, perspective, or form, they can better relay the complexity of issues important to them.

Multimodal

Multimodal papers and projects infuse new media into the composition process. Like multigenre composition, multimodal authoring includes the layering of different modes when creating digital texts, such as an integration of image, color, videos, and voice recording to accompany writing. Multimodal compositions integrate visuals, sounds, text, cartoons, video games, songs, and animations in response to a unit focus, essential questions, or literary work(s). To construct digital texts, students can work in PowerPoint, or Book Creator can easily integrate voice recordings and images. Apps such as Educreations, Tablet, and Piktochart can also be helpful. Online presentation platforms such as Google Slides and Prezi are also options.

Why should teachers workshopping toward democracy and justice encourage multimodal composition? The multimodal format allows students to create texts in different sign systems. Frameworks that value only print writing limit the understanding of complex literacies. After all, print is only one of the many sign systems through which texts are produced and understood. When creating multimodal compositions, "teachers are able to take advantage of the diversity of students' literacies rather than focus only on what they can and cannot do as readers/writers of print" (Simon, 2007, p. 158). In a multimodal world, literate production entails more than words; it includes a multiplicity of sign systems, and our students *want* to produce texts in different formats, for different audiences and purposes.

Workshopping teachers can guide students to design and construct multimodal texts in ways that are culturally responsive and socially transformative. Multimodal projects can be culturally responsive when we encourage writers to interweave first languages and provide opportunities for building on students' linguistic strengths and community literacies. Multimodal compositions can be transformative when students explore topics from a range of perspectives, incorporate genres in both visual and print modes, and problematize and challenge inequities. Students can create texts that envision social change and use multiple modal genres to creatively transform and reconstruct our world while overturning the composition status quo.

How to Teach Writing for Justice

Workshopping teachers support the writing process through a variety of workshop structures, including mentor texts, writing plans, independent writing, writing circles, craft mini-lessons, and publishing opportunities.

Mentor texts are models written by both professional and student writers that provide examples of structure, craft, and technique. A mentor text can be any genre that provides inspiration, information, and guidance. Before writing in different modes or creating a multigenre/multimodal paper or project, I often share screencasts created and recorded by student writers from the previous year. In addition to providing professional models, I empower student voices as they mentor others, introducing and explaining their compositions.

Once students are more familiar with the mode(s) expected, they begin to plan. Planning begins with selecting a topic. In accordance with democratic conditions, students need to be free to choose their own topics related to the unit focus or essential questions. Throughout the unit, workshopping teachers direct students' attention to the outside world, which can prompt ideas for composing. Chapman et al. (2011) guide students to question, What concerns you? Which of these issues concern your families and communities? Do these same issues distress the world on a global level (p. 540)? Likewise, Bomer and Bomer (2001) nudge student writing, asking, What do you want to speak publicly about? What things need to be addressed in your classroom, your school, your apartment building, your neighborhood, the city, the country, the world? In their unit focused on Beliefs, Values, and *Antigone*, Michael, Katie, and Josh encouraged students to write about a belief they would like to implement or change, with an emphasis on social justice (see Appendix C). Michael also provided students with a mentor text he wrote as a model for inspiration.

While workshopping, teachers want students to write about issues important to them and their communities, but we need to be patient and recognize that for students who live and learn at the margins of public schools, the transition from marginalized to empowered does not occur quickly or easily. Teachers need to thoughtfully scaffold students, helping them first understand writing as participation in a democratic process. We want to build students' trust in this basic premise: "You have things to say; there are ways to be heard; your voice matters in a conversation" (Ehst & Caskey, 2018, p. 39). While we encourage students to draw on personal experiences and real-world problems as a starting point, we know some students may not be ready to broach vulnerable topics (Ehst & Caskey, 2018).

Once students have found their topics, they begin to organize ideas. Writing plans can take any form: a web, a list, a chart, notes, an outline, a graphic organizer, a storyboard. The structure for the plan is influenced by the mode(s) of discourse. After planning, teachers provide uninterrupted and unencumbered time for students to write independently.

While students are drafting, they need opportunities to talk about what they are writing. A social justice approach to writing creates solidarity among peers and provides opportunities for students to respond to and embrace supportive criticism of their work (Chapman et al., 2011). Writing circles (Vopat, 2009) are small groups of students who gather to respond to one another's writing throughout a unit. We know students are more proactive with revision when they are regularly able to ask others for feedback, and writing circles can become supportive learning communities. Students bring questions and drafts to the circles, which gather regularly throughout a unit to support the writer through the process.

As students are drafting, revising, and editing, workshopping teachers provide support through mini-lessons. A craft mini-lesson directs students to make observations about the ways in which a text is written. Noden (1999), Anderson (2005, 2007), and Anderson and Dean (2014) use authentic and accessible text to draw student attention to grammar and style. Robb (2012) offers guidance for mini-lessons on strong verbs, specific nouns, show-don't-tell, figurative language, dialogue, direct quotations, paragraphing, transition sentences, sentence openings, run-ons, faulty pronoun references, punctuating complex sentences, using prepositional phrases, and comma usage. When we teach craft mini-lessons, our students learn to read like writers and write like readers.

Teachers also support the workshop writing process when they provide opportunities to publish writing. As Morrell (2008) reminds us, "We need to reconsider the reasons that students write in our classrooms, . . . the nature (genres) of the texts produced, and what happens to these texts once they are produced" (p. 86). When writing for democracy and justice, students are encouraged to produce texts for real audiences. They can create brochures, websites, editorials, public service announcements, research reports, and speeches that can be distributed to authentic venues beyond the school, such as newspaper editors, government officials, company CEOs, and internet websites. Students can share what they have learned with people in the community, including teachers, school administrators, and community leaders. When students present their modes of discourse to others, they not only perceive themselves as writers, but they also begin to believe in the power of their words to create positive change in their communities.

Chapter Summary

Workshopping teachers support students in writing about issues of justice and injustice in the word and the world. We practice a socially oriented approach to the teaching of writing and engage students in writing based on issues raised in the texts we read and reflected in our communities. Students write narrative, informational/explanatory, and argumentative texts throughout a focus unit as they question their reading and clarify meaning. We also encourage writing in various culminating genres related to social issues, everyday justice, power relationships, and other social, cultural, historical, political, or socioeconomical topics related to the unit focus and essential questions. Students create a culminating narrative, informative/explanatory (e.g., list, summary, description, process, definition, comparison-contrast, classification, cause-effect, problem-solution), argumentative, literary, or multigenre/multimodal paper or project to demonstrate their thinking. Workshopping teachers challenge dominant written Discourse (Gee, 1989) with multigenre and multimodal writing and support the writing process through a variety of workshop structures, including mentor texts, writing plans, independent writing, writing circles, craft mini-lessons, and publishing opportunities.

8

Supporting Inquiry and Agency

It's one of the simplest sentences in the world, just four words, but they're the four hugest words in the world when they're put together.
You can do it.
I can do it.
Let's do it.

—Sherman Alexie, *The Absolutely True Diary of a Part-Time Indian*

Workshopping teachers support student inquiry and agency. We challenge students to question the status quo, envision the word differently, and do something about it. Chapter 8 introduces why and how to engage students in research and action necessary for social change.

When we apply a social justice framework to teaching, we have a goal to do something. Once students have inquired into a social issue, they plan a feasible course of action. In the spirit of Dewey and Freire, workshopping teachers prepare students for responsible citizenship, helping them play a role in a democracy as they make efforts to change their world.

Workshopping students engage in inquiry and activism toward a greater societal and global good.

Supporting Student Inquiry

Workshopping teachers prompt students to read about issues of justice, equity, diversity, and inclusion; question power in the word and the world; talk about local or global issues; listen to diverse opinions and perspectives; and write critically about matters important to them. We encourage and guide inquiry through our curriculum and pedagogy. Morrell (2008) proposed several core tenets of critical composition pedagogy that support inquiry:

1. Historicity. Begin with students' experiences as citizens of the world.
2. Problem-posing. Embrace, as curriculum, real-world problems and struggles of marginalized people in the world.
3. Dialogic. Entail authentic humanizing interactions with people in the world.
4. Emancipatory. Confront individual alienation and social injustice and have as its project liberation from oppressive realities.
5. Praxis. Be about action and reflection upon that action. (p. 116)

Teachers want to hold to these precepts as we prepare students for social action.

Workshopping teachers center experiences to promote critical inquiry into relevant issues, encouraging students to identify and respond to issues of justice and injustice in their lives. We work to reposition students as active learners and knowledge producers as they inquire into issues of inequity in their schools and communities, asking students the following: What social issues have you become more aware of throughout this unit? What is bothering you about your local and global communities? Engaging in personal inquiry leads students to research and propels them into the world.

Kayla, for example, challenges students to research issues important to them, inspired by the literature read across the year. As mentioned in Chapter 2, students in Kayla's English I class read Jason Reynolds and Brendan Kiely's *All American Boys*, Walter Dean Myers's *Monster*, David Pelzer's *A Child Called "It,"* Laurie Halse Anderson's *Speak*, Sherman Alexie's *The Absolutely True Diary of a Part-Time Indian*, Ishmael Beah's *A Long Way Gone*, George Orwell's *Animal Farm*, John Steinbeck's *Of Mice and Men*, Angie Thomas's *The Hate U Give*, John Boyne's *The Boy in the Striped Pajamas*, and a selection of short stories from Jimmy Santiago Baca's *Stories from the Edge*. In response to their reading, students conduct an independent inquiry around a topic of their choice (see Appendix D).

Kayla supports students throughout the research and writing process. Students collaboratively brainstorm a list of what they would like to see changed in their communities. They take field trips to the library and learn how to locate, evaluate, and annotate sources. They ask permission before gathering data through surveys and interviews. Over the past few years, Kayla's students have researched the Black Lives Matter movement, police brutality, effects of poverty on children, storm water pollution, mental health during COVID-19, discrimination and violence against LGBTQ+ students, the school-to-prison pipeline, AIDS, domestic violence, gun violence, women's reproductive rights, rape, and the Dakota Access Pipeline protests.

More than one teacher has fostered student inquiry after reading Jason Reynolds and Brendan Kiely's *All American Boys*. Courtney and Hannah, inspired by lessons found on the Learning for Justice website (www.learningforjustice.org/classroom-resources/lessons/digital-activism-remixed-hashtags-for-voice-visibility-and-visions-of), had students create a #activism project (see Figure 11) in which they explore different social media hashtag campaigns related to issues of justice, equity, diversity, and inclusion. Rodesiler (2018) also offers examples of relevant inquiry projects inspired by reading *All American Boys*. In this class, students researched incidents of police violence, interrogated media representations of athletes who have protested police violence, studied judicial rulings about students' rights to protest, investigated local reactions to athletes protesting police violence, examined other historical sports-related protests, and explored the lives of athletes throughout history who embraced activism. To prompt student inquiry and guide research, Nicole has students answer a series of questions (see Figure 12). These questions guide students through their initial inquiry process.

All American Boys Activism Project:
Hashtags for Voice, Visibility, and Visions of Social Justice

Research (major assessment)
Complete the chart as you explore different social media hashtag campaigns related to themes of identity, diversity, justice, and social action. The first hashtag, #BlackLivesMatter, will be modeled for you!

Hashtag	Founder(s) and Year Created (If Known)	Purpose?	Related to Justice, Equity, Diversity, Inclusion?	Intended Audience	At least 2 Comments or Connections or Questions
#BlackLivesMatter					
#					
#					
#					
#					

FIGURE 11. *All American Boys* #Activism Project.

Identify the Scope of Your Research

You may not need to address all of the questions below, but these are some ways to start thinking about the scope of your inquiry. What is the story around this issue?

- **What is the issue?**
- **Why does it need to be addressed?**
- **What do you hope to accomplish?**
- **Historical Background: What is the evolution of this issue?**
  - What are important statistics we should know?
  - What are some historical examples of why this issue matters?
  - What are the defining terms we must understand to consider this issue?
  - Is this issue the cause of a problem or the effect of a larger problem? For example, hunger, homelessness, and some forms of crime are symptoms of poverty, so any long-term lasting change must address the causes of poverty, not just the outcomes (hunger, homelessness, crime).
- **Stakeholders: Who are the stakeholders for this issue? Who has been in conflict?**
  - **Community activists.** People who have worked for change on this and/or other issues and have demonstrated their commitment to the community.
  - **Local officials, including policymakers.** They may be the policymakers themselves, or they may have some say over funding or other aspects of any eventual intervention.
  - **Community members and groups who are affected by this issue.** These might include parents, seniors, landowners, environmentalists, or even the whole community.
  - **Experts and researchers in the field.** These folks can add to the credibility of the final result.
  - **Best practices: What are the best practices for addressing this issue? What has worked elsewhere?**

FIGURE 12. Nicole's questions to help students identify the scope of research.

What We Know about I-Search

A helpful format that allows students to demonstrate their inquiry and research is the I-Search. These papers or projects are student focused and encourage writing about a researcher's journey. More process oriented than a traditional research paper, an I-Search shares the details of how a student has come to discover something new.

Macrorie (1988) defines the steps of the I-Search process as the following:

- Allow your topic to choose you.
- Find people: locate experts or authorities.
- Read as much as you can about your topic before you actually meet people.

- Interview people who know a lot about your topic.
- Test the statements of experts against those of other experts.
- Consult firsthand sources.
- Tell your search as a story.

In I-Search projects, I have had students ask: Why aren't there many students of color in AP courses? What are "American" dreams? How are students treated differently when shopping at the mall? Do teachers discipline students differently based on race, gender, sexual identity, and/or socioeconomic status?

Once students have completed their inquiry journeys, they write up the process of their research. Rather than focus solely on the products or answers to questions, they share the details of their process. Not so easily found on the web or generated by ChatGPT, these first-person narratives detail why a topic is important and what a student initially knows about the topic, how they researched the topic, and what they learned about the topic. Macrorie (1988) suggests the following format for the I-Search:

- What I knew (and didn't know about my topic when I started out)
- Why I'm writing this paper (here's where a real need should show up; the writer demonstrates that the search may make a difference in their life)
- The search (story of the hunt)
- What I learned (or didn't learn—a search that failed can be as exciting and valuable as one that succeeded)

Students document the story of their research process from beginning to end, relating the search to self. Of course, students can also represent the products of their inquiry through any genre, especially multigenre and multimodal projects and papers, introduced in Chapter 7.

Supporting Student Agency

Once students have engaged in inquiry and research, they often begin to think about ways to promote change. An enlightened consciousness nudges them forward to take action in the world. The teaching of language arts and literacy has gained a social and civic purpose. Grounded in the theories of Dewey and Freire, workshopping teachers prepare students for responsible citizenship, helping them assume an active role in a participatory democracy. We encourage students to "stand, speak and act" for justice on behalf of democracy (Williams, 2004). When we embrace social justice in our classrooms, we declare that we're all responsible for improving our world (Schmidt, 2009).

As described in previous chapters, teachers workshop for democracy and justice by deconstructing texts related to various social issues. While we want students to deconstruct the word, we also want them to reconstruct the world by looking for opportunities in their communities to take action against injustice, thereby transferring critical reading into some type of social action. As we all know, high school students rarely accept injustice as the status quo; they know instinctively when something is unfair. Storm and Rainey (2018) define *woke* as being "aware of systemic injustice and ways of interrupting injustice and . . . feel[ing] able to participate in making change" (p. 95). Woke students take action to address social and political issues raised by texts. Woke teachers encourage students to act and move critical stances from the word to the world.

Social action projects reflect a commitment to schooling for democracy. As Greene (1995) explains, democratic education "involves provoking persons to get up from their seats" and use their voices with vigor (p. 72). When we teach English for social justice, we blur the lines between teaching and activism (Bruce, 2013, p. 32). Workshopping teachers move learning outside and engage students in projects at the community, state, and even global levels.

Social action projects differ from community service projects in that community service projects such as volunteering are often wrought with false understandings of need, social policy, and empowerment because they lack planning or collaboration between the helpers and the helped (Stachowiak, 2017). Social action involves the students and the community working in tandem from planning to implementation, focuses on tackling the root causes of a specific social issue, and educates for sustainable social and/or political change. These projects reach beyond helping others to actively assist in dismantling systems of privilege, power, and oppression.

Students engage in social action projects when they address events, actions, or people that students deem to be discriminatory or antidemocratic and attempt to alter their trajectory (Boyd, 2017). Social action projects begin with inquiry as students select a social issue to focus on. This can be a local issue such as high rent in their neighborhoods or a more global issue such as access to the COVID-19 vaccine. Students can work independently or collaboratively as they engage in research around their topic, defining and contextualizing. Ultimately, students create print and/or visual texts that highlight their civic voices, identify possibilities for change, and offer a feasible course of action.

Teachers have incorporated social action into their classrooms in various ways. Some actions are more direct than others. Simmons (2012) incorporated the Hunger Games trilogy into her classroom to encourage students to inquire into issues of violence and domination in our world, relating them to the injustices faced by the twelve districts of the fictional Panem. She prompted students to compare the Capitol's wastefulness to that of the American population, to correlate forced labor in the districts with various types of involuntary employment around the world, to relate the idea of children set one against another in combat to the use of child soldiers in many African countries, and likened Finnick's description of how victors are sold as sex objects with the booming sex trafficking industry that occurs in all major countries. Once they are fired up (pun intended), students select a topic, engage in inquiry around that topic, and take action, some addressing hunger and planting a garden for the school, others using a school assembly to raise student awareness about the mining of conflict diamonds in Sierra Leone.

Kayla's students always transform their initial inquiry into action. After students have completed their research, she shares examples of how previous students have heightened awareness and prompted change. Students create a visual display around their research topic and raise their civic voices at a research fair, talking with community members about their papers and distributing a handout about their topics. Kayla invites school district officials, college professors, city council members, and other community stakeholders. This past year, the mayor showed up!

For those students who want to continue to develop their projects, Kayla introduces NextGen (http://breadloafnextgen.middcreate.net/), a youth advocacy group she sponsors, and encourages students to attend meetings. The Bread Loaf Teacher Network's NextGen is a youth social action network linking seven sites across the nation, including Lawrence, Massachusetts; Atlanta, Georgia; Aiken, South Carolina; Louisville, Kentucky; Vermont; the Navajo Nation, and the Santa Fe Indian School. Launched by a two-year grant from the Ford Foundation to the Middlebury Bread Loaf School of English, NextGen mobilizes social justice teams to address issues that youth have identified as significant. Kayla recalls a group of students who started an after-school program to combat gang recruitment in their neighborhood:

> Dale, RJ, and Rashaad were freshmen in my 7th period English I class. They were all basketball players and ready to be "done" with school by the time they reached my classroom. When they were introduced to the research projects, they quickly paired up. When I asked them to think about what they would like to see changed in their community, Dale quickly responded, "I don't want the gangs to recruit my younger brother." Rashaad added that the gangs in their neighborhood are "bad" and "always getting the younger guys." I asked them how they avoided being in

> the gangs. They responded with, "basketball." Because they were good players, they got left alone. I asked if they wanted to focus on gangs directly, but they told me this was too dangerous. They decided they wanted to focus on the lack of positive mentors for young black males in their community. They did the research, wrote their paper, made contacts, and did their presentation. After the research unit was done, they decided they wanted to start a basketball mentor program and continue to take action. During the same time, Bread Loaf School of English reached out to sponsor a youth advocacy group in my town.
>
> I suggested Dale, RJ, and Rashaad start the group and promote change in the community. They were all in. This support helped them continue their research project that began in class. Bread Loaf School of English helped sponsor their project, providing monetary support and a network of resources to help them plan and implement action. The boys partnered with a neighboring elementary school and structured an after-school program. The program focused on kids that lived in Dale's neighborhood. The school provided bus transportation. Bread Loaf provided food and supplies. Their program offered: homework help, arts/crafts, basketball skills, mentoring talks, outside games, and dinner. The program ran from 2:45pm–5:00pm. The boys recruited 15 other teens to help with the program, mostly basketball players, and 40 elementary students attended.
>
> After the first year and even after the boys graduated, the program has continued (except for last year due to COVID-19). The partnership has remained, and Dale, RJ, and Rashaad have trained other teens to take their place. Although, they all still tend to show up at the after-school program.

Ryan's school has adopted the Expeditionary Learning education model (https://eleducation.org/), which connects learning to real-world issues and embraces core practices that include supporting global citizenship. Teachers and student leaders design lessons that value and strive for justice, equity, diversity, and inclusion as well as those that enable students to make concrete contributions to the world around them. Through "expeditions," students engage in fieldwork and become active investigators, applying research tools and techniques of inquiry, engaging with experts from the community, and enacting standards of presentation used by professionals in the field.

During their senior year, students in Ryan's "crew" engaged in an expedition designed to meet the following learning targets: *I can collaborate with my crew, through discussion, research, and fieldwork experiences, to create a positive and lasting impact on our local community; I can collaborate with my crew by experiencing and proposing solutions for a local social issue in order to become a more productive global citizen; I can participate in activities that illustrate the habits of scholarship and citizenship, and show high-quality evidence of my participation.* To meet these learning targets, students explored a social issue of their choice through authentic experiences in order to make an impact on their issue and present at the school's Learning Impact Conference.

One particular group of students—Mariah, Gabbie, Allie, Ethan, and Carson—conducted their research on Alzheimer's disease. Through their inquiry, they discovered the powerful effect music can have on stimulating response and memory. They met with a psychology professor from a local university and learned more about how memories are formed. They discovered that while medication for Alzheimer's patients can help prevent the buildup of protein plaques, medicines work best with nondrug therapies, including music therapy. The students visited a local assisted living community specializing in Alzheimer's and dementia care and met with the lead activities director for the Alzheimer's wing. They spent some time getting to know the patients and realized how important it is to be familiar with meaningful songs in the patients' lives. In repeat visits, the students played the patients' favorite music, and the responses were incredibly positive. After they played Elvis songs for an older woman named Annie, she began to engage in conversation with a staff member, Sarah, about Elvis. Sarah recalls: "She [Annie] was talking about Elvis obsessively, similar to a teenager fangirling over their celebrity crush." Sarah told the group on their way out that Annie had not talked a lot lately and they had been concerned about her. But she lit up once again when hearing the Elvis songs, almost as though something had just "clicked in her mind." In their presentation at the school's Impact Conference, the group shared video of Annie dancing and remembering.

A group of students in Nicole's class, inspired by Tom Robinson in Harper Lee's *To Kill a Mockingbird,* focused their inquiry on the effects of racism on the justice system in the South. They selected and studied the George Stinney case. George Stinney was a fourteen-year-old African American boy who was convicted of the murder of two young white girls in Alcolu, South Carolina. In 1944 Stinney was the youngest person in US history to be executed. He did not commit the crime for which he was convicted; his conviction was a result of racism, not evidence of his guilt.

In 2014, in part because of the research conducted by Nicole's students, the state of South Carolina was forced to admit that Stinney was wrongly convicted. The students contacted the attorney who had filed to have the case reopened in South Carolina and asked how they could help. They did basic clerk work for the case, reading primary documents and raising questions about the evidence. They met with the Stinney family legal team, interviewed living relatives, and educated the general public about the case. They presented their findings all over the state, speaking with school groups, church groups, and rotary clubs.

In December 2014, the judge finally ruled that the State of South Carolina did not provide Stinney with his due process, and in the summer of 2015, Nicole's students were invited to Alcolu by Stinney's family for the dedication of the first memorial to commemorate his short life. In the past several years, Nicole's students have chosen to work on vacating an unjust conviction, proposing legislation related to the rights of sex-trafficking victims, and calling for reform to current laws that punish juveniles for certain types of sexting by putting them on the sex offender registry for life.

Caroline and Stephanie, inspired by Gallagher and Kittle (2018), leveraged student writing for agency. As a culminating unit project, students wrote letters to a government official. Students were required to research a specific issue or policy they felt passionate about and to write a professional letter to the appropriate federal legislative representative. Students were given the following writing guidelines: state your chosen social justice/advocacy issue; concisely state your position regarding the issue; explain at least two reasons supporting your position; and state the action you would like the representative to take. Caroline created an online choice board that guided student inquiry around various topics, including public health, school policy, LGBTQ+, BLM, immigration, and homelessness. Students were given time to research and locate information that supported their stance on the issue. They were also given smaller activities, including mini-lessons on ethos, logos, and pathos, to scaffold their thinking into a more critical mindset.

While each preceding example is unique, they share common threads of inquiry and agency interweaving student efforts to promote positive change in their world.

How to Guide Student Agency

A variety of processes can be implemented to guide students through social action. Boyd (2017, p. 102) uses a framework for direct action that involves four steps: contextualizing, organizing, acting, and reflecting (COAR). Students locate an issue and deeply examine its context, engaging in research by examining multiple perspectives and viewpoints. Next, students plan and organize the actions needed to address the injustice. They then take action. Finally, students reflect on the process and plan for future successes and challenges.

Similarly, Pedraza and Rodriguez (2018) introduce students to critical praxis as a way to take action against a structure to be transformed. The five steps of the critical praxis model include identifying a problem; researching the problem; developing a collective plan of action to address the problem; implementing the collective plan of action; and evaluating the action, assessing its efficacy, and reexamining the state of the problem.

In Nicole's class, student civic agency is guided and supported. After engaging in inquiry and research around their chosen issue (see Figure 12), students design a first-person advocacy proposal (see Figure 13). After completing the proposal, Nicole's students complete a community outreach plan (see Figure 14), which is used to educate the broader public about their chosen issue. Students then offer their presentation to other local schools, host a town hall for the general public, and speak at the legislative children's committee meeting (most states have such a committee, and testimony is open for anyone who wishes to offer it).

First-Person Advocacy Proposal

An **advocacy proposal** is a researched persuasive argument, often delivered as a speech. Once you have identified your scope of change and audience, you're ready to craft your first-person advocacy proposal. First-person advocacy proposals are used in the following contexts:

- Legislation testimony at the Joint Citizens and Legislative Committee on Children and as subcommittee hearings come up in our state legislature. In South Carolina, public input is only accepted at the subcommittee level.
- Community forums can be in-person, virtual live, or asynchronous social media/online.

How can you tell the story of how the issue impacts you/your community in a way that promotes positive change? While you will likely deliver your first-person advocacy proposal as a speech, writing it out beforehand allows you to plan your words carefully so that your communication is as effective as it can be and you feel prepared and confident.

1. **Introduce yourself and explain why you are speaking to this specific audience:** Thank you for allowing me to speak with you today. My name is ________ and I live in ________. I am speaking to you today to ________. This issue is important to me because ________.
    - Outline what precisely you want others to do. Is there a bill you wish to see passed? Is it an educational project for your peers? This would include a timeline of events and any resources necessary for the project's success.
2. **Demonstrate your research and your understanding of impact. Use both factual evidence and personal story/anecdotes to support your proposal.**
    - Factual evidence, including ones that address any misconceptions about the issue.
    - Personal story/anecdotes that demonstrate impact, both of the issue unaddressed and addressed.
    - Acknowledge the challenges but point to the evidence for positive change.
    - This would help people by ________.
3. **Conclusion: Restate/review your position at the end of your testimony and thank your audience for the time to speak.**
4. **Preparation:**
    - Anticipate questions you might be asked that challenge your argument.
    - Rehearse enough so that the words come easily to you, not so that you are delivering something memorized but that it's easy for you to talk about it. One way to prepare is to write down the bullet points of your speech after you've written it.
    - A strong speech is responsive to your audience. You might find your audience reacts to one part of your speech and that you want to say more/less than you'd originally planned. The more confident you feel in your knowledge and preparation, the better able you will be to adjust in the moment as needed.

FIGURE 13. Nicole's directions for a first-person advocacy proposal.

Community Education Outreach Plan

Create a presentation that begins with a problem statement, provides evidence of the immediacy of the issue, and includes what can be done about the issue and what the viewer particularly can do to affect change. Always include a multimedia component: Choose 1–2 clips we should view to give us greater access to understanding this issue. The clips should be no longer than 2–3 minutes each and may be news sources, documentary clips, or opinion pieces. This helps visually stimulate the audience. Be sure to use effective hashtags for cataloguing and "following" algorithms to amplify messages; learn how to leverage public opinion to extend the reach of conversations and further build community.

FIGURE 14. Nicole's community education outreach plan.

There are many examples of students making a difference that teachers can use for inspiration and guidance. Nicole scavenges the news for examples of young people offering positive models of civic engagement. She has used Stella Keating's testimonial at the Senate Judiciary Committee Hearing on March 17 for the Equality Act for LGBTQ Rights; Grace Miller's Children's Committee testimony on relationship violence; Reilly Arford's Children's Committee testimony on human trafficking; and Jada Adams's Children's Committee testimony on arts funding in schools. These are all uplifting examples of real people engaged in meaningful struggle. Along with the many examples found on YouTube and TED Talks (e.g., Greta Thunberg, Malala Yousafzai), books that encourage and spotlight the work of young change agents, such as Phillip Hoose's *It's Our World, Too! Stories of Young People Who Are Making a Difference,* Maureen Johnson's *How I Resist: Activism and Hope for a New Generation,* and Jamie Margolin's *Youth to Power: Your Voice and How to Use It*, can help students realize that they can effect positive change. Other resources I have found helpful in supporting student agency are the Learning for Justice (www.learningforjustice.org/) and DoSomething (www.dosomething.org/us) websites.

What Is Critical Research?

When our students engage in inquiry related to critical theory and praxis, they are answering Morrell's (2009) call for critical research. Critical research is the study of turning critical theory(ies) into practice. Investigators design, implement, and study humanizing literacy classroom practices, seeking to answer questions including, How do we know what students are learning? And how can we find out? Critical research honors local knowledge and is conducted by those most affected—students, teachers, and university researchers alike. After all, teachers and students are key stakeholders in education and deserve to play a role in addressing oppressive conditions and imagining radical possibilities in classrooms and schools. The critical research process is a systematic, evidence-based, locally initiated approach and is intended to enact positive academic identity and social outcomes. Participants and stakeholders are involved in the critical research design as well as in data collection and analysis. As Morrell (2008, p. 132) argues, we need to "democratize the tools of research" and encourage students to become critical researchers as part of the development of their own critical literacies.

Morrell (2009) shares two examples of how students, teachers, and university researchers have used critical research to design and analyze innovative classroom curricula and pedagogies. In the first example, students wrote narratives about their daily lives inside and outside of school, making connections between their individual lives and the social conditions that reproduce inequity. Students were introduced to social theory that they then used to develop critiques of an equitable school. Through research, they came to a greater understanding of the oppressive social, political, and material conditions that made life more difficult for them and others while also seeing themselves as agents with the potential to change these conditions. They moved from translating their own experiences to making statements about the role of schools in promoting social inequality.

In the second example, youth worked with teachers and university researchers as critical sociologists who collected data on the dropout problem in their city. Alongside teachers, students in research groups developed a research question, designed a research study, collected and analyzed data, wrote essays and research reports, created PowerPoint presentations, produced short documentary films, and shared their final products at City Hall with the mayor's Office of Education.

Becoming Agents for Change

When teachers engage in critical research with students, we become agents for change because we dare to imagine a new way of researching. When teachers workshop for democracy and justice, we become agents for change because we dare to imagine a new way of teaching. Teacher change agents accept that they have a role in creating different and better ways.

Teachers need to be agents for change alongside students. As Mundorf et al. (2019) remind us, we have a long history of working toward societal change. Black educators in the Jim Crow South acted as "secret social justice advocates" (Smathers Library Gallery, 2018), and LGBTQ+ teachers fought the National

Education Association to have a voice and structure in the union (Graves, 2015). More recently, #DisruptTexts (Ebarvia et al., 2018), teach-ins at the United States–Mexico border (Camera, 2019), and teacher walkouts (Catte et al., 2018) are just a few examples of teachers fighting injustice.

Teachers can promote change in their classrooms, schools, districts, and communities through their curricular, pedagogical, and social actions. Inside classrooms, teachers can demonstrate agency through teaching a justice-oriented curriculum and practicing democratic pedagogy. Appendix E offers an example of teachers promoting change through a critical workshopping curriculum and pedagogy. In this short narrative, Sarah, Anna Maria, and Bridges describe how they teach George Orwell's *Animal Farm* and Samira Ahmed's *Internment* through a unit focus on the Corruption of Power.

When we workshop the canon for democracy and justice, we become what Postman and Weingartner (1970) refer to as "soft revolutionaries," working within school systems, making large changes and "simple improvements" when possible, knowing that small changes over time can eventually lead to a new system (p. 4). Workshopping teachers wear a pragmatic hat. We are well aware of current realities, yet we simultaneously see beyond them. Yes, wearing a pragmatic hat may involve the teaching of certain canonical texts; however, we also don a more radical hat that allows us to reimagine traditional curricula and pedagogy. Workshopping teachers are "radical pragmatist(s)" (Duncan-Andrade & Morrell, 2008, p. 167).

With this book, I have integrated new ideas with old, interweaving critical literacy theory within a workshop curriculum and practice. While this book is not radical enough, it will guide you to make changes with your current curriculum and pedagogy. Writing this book has been my own small act of agency. I have written my way through two pandemics. Yes, I personally recognize the challenges teachers face when asked to enact their own agency—the realities of limited time, materials, and resources, not to mention growing national and federal pressure to conform to institutional policies and practices regarding curriculum and practice. But I also know that teachers *want* to be agents of change. No one I know became a teacher for the money. I believe teachers to be change agents with the vision to imagine new ways of doing things for a more just tomorrow, even if for now these changes exist only in our individual classrooms or departments. As we know, every wave begins with a ripple. Small classroom changes can lead to larger systemic changes. There is much to do.

You can do it.

I can do it.

Let's do it.

Chapter Summary

Workshopping for democracy and justice engages students in inquiry and activism toward a greater societal and global good. Workshopping teachers center students' experiences and perspectives to promote critical inquiry into relevant issues inspired by literature, encouraging students to identify and respond to issues of justice and injustice in their lives and communities. Social action projects begin with inquiry as students select a social issue on which to focus. Students work independently or collaboratively as they engage in research around their topics. Ultimately, students create print and/or visual texts that highlight their civic voices, identify possibilities for change, and offer a feasible course of action.

Social action projects reflect a commitment to schooling for democracy. There are processes to guide students through social action, and teachers use examples of students making a difference that spotlight the work of young change agents. Teachers have incorporated social action into their classrooms in various ways, some actions being more direct than others. When our students engage in inquiry related to critical theory and praxis, they are engaging in critical research. Critical research is the study of turning critical theory(ies) into practice.

Teachers need to be agents for change alongside students. Teachers can promote change in their classrooms, schools, districts, and communities through their curricular, pedagogical, and social actions. We can demonstrate agency through teaching a justice-oriented curriculum and practicing democratic pedagogy—through workshopping the canon for democracy and justice.

Appendixes

Appendix A

Sample Units with Canonical Texts, Contemporary Texts, Unit Foci, Critical Essential Questions, and Supplementary Texts

Canonical Texts	Contemporary Texts	Unit Focus	Critical Essential Questions	Sample Supplementary Texts
Geoffrey Chaucer, "General Prologue," *The Canterbury Tales* Anne Frank, *Diary of a Young Girl* Franz Kafka, *The Metamorphosis* Ovid, *Metamorphoses* J. D. Salinger, *The Catcher in the Rye* William Shakespeare, *Hamlet* Robert Louis Stevenson, *Strange Case of Dr. Jekyll and Mr. Hyde* Oscar Wilde, *The Picture of Dorian Gray*	Chinua Achebe, *Things Fall Apart* Sherman Alexie, *The Absolutely True Diary of a Part-Time Indian* Sandra Cisneros, *The House on Mango Street* Stephen Collins, *The Gigantic Beard That Was Evil* April Daniels, *Dreadnought* Debby Dahl Edwardson, *My Name Is Not Easy* Sharon G. Flake, *The Skin I'm In* Nikki Grimes, *Bronx Masquerade* Adib Khorram, *Darius the Great Is Not Okay* David Levithan, *Every Day* Wes Moore, *The Other Wes Moore: One Name, Two Fates* Walter Dean Myers, *Monster* Matt de la Peña, *Mexican WhiteBoy* Meredith Russo, *If I Was Your Girl* Benjamin Alire Sáenz, *Aristotle and Dante Discover the Secrets of the Universe* Ozge Samanci, *Dare to Disappoint: Growing Up in Turkey*	**Identities and Perspectives**	Who am I? How are identities shaped? Is identity constant? What is the relationship between identities, perspectives, and power?	**Short Stories** Avi, *What Do Fish Have to Do with Anything?* Michael Cart (ed.), *How Beautiful the Ordinary: Twelve Stories of Identity* Sandra Cisneros, "My Name" Donald R. Gallo (ed.), *No Easy Answers: Short Stories about Teenagers Making Tough Choices* Jamaica Kincaid, "Girl" Flannery O'Connor, "Good Country People" Alice Walker, "Everyday Use" Ibi Zoboi (ed.), *Black Enough: Stories of Being Young and Black in America* **Informational Texts** CommonLit Staff, "Freud's Theory of the Id, Ego, and Superego" Rob Dekkers, "Influencers and Identity: Who Do You Want to Be?" Al Desetta (ed.), *The Courage to Be Yourself: True Stories by Teens about Cliques, Conflicts, and Overcoming Peer Pressure* Saul McLeod, "Classical Conditioning"

Canonical Texts	Contemporary Texts	Unit Focus	Critical Essential Questions	Sample Supplementary Texts
	Erika L. Sánchez, *I Am Not Your Perfect Mexican Daughter* Marjane Satrapi, *Persepolis: The Story of a Childhood* Rachel Vincent, *Brave New Girl* Renée Watson, *Piecing Me Together* G. Willow Wilson & Adrian Alphona, *Ms. Marvel, Vol.1: No Normal* (Ms. Marvel Series) Gene Luen Yang, *American Born Chinese*			Saul McLeod, "Self-Concept" Nausicaa Renner, "How Social Media Shapes Our Identity" Youth Communication, *Starting with "I": Personal Essays by Teenagers* **Picture Books** Marie Bradby & Chris Soentpiet, *Mama, Where Are You From?* Yangsook Choi, *The Name Jar* Marguerite W. Davol & Irene Trivas, *Black, White, Just Right!* Sheila Hamanaka, *All the Colors of the Earth* Joanna Ho & Dung Ho, *Eyes That Kiss in the Corners* Langston Hughes & Charles R. Smith Jr., *My People* Dinah Johnson & Kelly Johnson, *Hair Dance!* Kyo Maclear & Isabelle Arsenault, *Spork* Ibtihaj Muhammad & Hatem Aly, *The Proudest Blue: A Story of Hijab and Family* Sandra L. Pinkney & Miles C. Pinkney, *I Am Latino: The Beauty in Me* David Shannon, *A Bad Case of Stripes* **Poetry** Emily Dickinson, "I'm Nobody! Who Are You?" Paul Laurence Dunbar, "We Wear the Mask" Betsy Franco (ed.), *Things I Have to Tell You: Poems and Writing by Teenage Girls* Langston Hughes, "Motto" Audre Lorde, "Hanging Fire" Edwin Arlington Robinson, "Richard Cory" Walt Whitman, *Song of Myself* Karenne Wood, "My Standard Response"

Canonical Texts	Contemporary Texts	Unit Focus	Critical Essential Questions	Sample Supplementary Texts
				Jacqueline Woodson, *Brown Girl Dreaming* WritersCorp, *Paint Me Like I Am: Teen Poems from WritersCorps* **Music** Christina Aguilera, "Reflection" The Beatles, "I'm Looking through You" Edie Brickell & New Bohemians, "What I Am" James Brown, "Papa's Got a Brand New Bag" Pearl Jam, "Who You Are" Olivia Rodrigo, "The Rose Song" Sly & the Family Stone, "Everyday People" The Who, "Who Are You" **TV/Film** *Boy Erased* *Finding Your Roots with Henry Louis Gates, Jr.* **Plays** Allison Green, *Anonymous* Jon Jory & Jason Pizzarello, *Identity Play; or Who You Are If You Think You Are* **Photography** Brandon Stanton, *Humans* **Photoblog** Brandon Stanton, *Humans of New York*
Anne Frank, *Diary of a Young Girl* Harper Lee, *To Kill a Mockingbird* George Orwell, *1984* Sophocles, *Antigone*	Elizabeth Acevedo, *The Poet X* Samira Ahmed, *Internment* Becky Albertalli & Aisha Saeed, *Yes No Maybe So* Laurie Halse Anderson, *Speak* Candace Bushnell & Katie Cotugno, *Rules for Being a Girl* Brandy Colbert, *The Voting Booth* Robert Cormier, *The Chocolate War* Abi Daré, *The Girl with the Louding Voice*	**Voice and Agency**	When should we use our voice and act against injustice? What is the relationship between voice, agency, and power? How can we gain voice and act against injustice?	**Short Stories** Amnesty International UK (ed.), *Here I Stand: Stories That Speak for Freedom* Alexis Pauline Gumbs, "Evidence" Shirley Jackson, "The Lottery" Ra Page (ed.), *Protest: Stories of Resistance* **Informational Texts** Laurie Halse Anderson, *Shout* BBC News, "The Hong Kong Protests Explained in 100 and 500 Words"

Canonical Texts	Contemporary Texts	Unit Focus	Critical Essential Questions	Sample Supplementary Texts
	Whitney Gardner, *You're Welcome, Universe* Lois Lowry, *Number the Stars* William Kamkwamba & Bryan Mealer, *The Boy Who Harnessed the Wind: Creating Currents of Electricity and Hope* Ali Nijood, *I Am Nijood, Age 10 and Divorced* Jason Reynolds and Brendan Kiely, *All American Boys* Rafik Schami, *A Hand Full of Stars* Angie Thomas, *The Hate U Give* Aronya Waller, *Mama* Renée Watson & Ellen Hagan, *Watch Us Rise* Malala Yousafzai, *I Am Malala: How One Girl Stood Up for Education and Changed the World*			Marke Bieschke, *Into the Streets: A Young Person's Visual History of Protest in the United States* Tom Head, "Why Protest Events Are Not a Waste of Time" Maureen Johnson (ed.), *How I Resist: Activism and Hope for a New Generation* Patrisse Khan-Cullors & Asha Bandele, *When They Call You a Terrorist: A Story of Black Lives Matter and the Power to Change the World* (Young Adult Edition) Paige Leskin & Rosie Perper, "TikTok Issues Public Apology for Suspending the Account of the Teen behind the Viral Chinese Takedown Video Disguised as a Makeup Tutorial" Michael Long, *Kids on the March: 15 Stories of Speaking Out, Protesting, and Fighting for Justice* Jamie Margolin, *Youth to Power: Your Voice and How to Use It* Moisés Naím, "Why Street Protests Don't Work" KaeLyn Rich, *Girls Resist! A Guide to Activism, Leadership, and Starting a Revolution* Judith Vonberg, Atika Shubert & Nadine Schmidt, "Teen behind New Hijab Emoji: 'I Just Wanted an Emoji of Me'" Elie Wiesel, "Acceptance Speech on the Occasion of the Award of the Nobel Peace Prize" Dave Zirin, *The Kaepernick Effect: Taking a Knee, Changing the World*

Canonical Texts	Contemporary Texts	Unit Focus	Critical Essential Questions	Sample Supplementary Texts
				<u>Picture Books</u> Jeannine Atkins & Venantius J. Pinto, *Aani and the Tree Huggers* Kenneth Braswell, Joe Dent & Julie Anderson, *Daddy, There's a Noise Outside* Don Brown, *Kid Blink Beats the World* Eve Bunting, *Terrible Things: An Allegory of the Holocaust* Doreen Cronin & Betsy Lewin, *Click, Clack, Moo: Cows That Type* Drew Daywalt & Oliver Jeffers, *The Day the Crayons Quit* Carmen Agra Deedy & Eugene Yelchin, *The Rooster Who Would Not Be Quiet!* Leticia Hernández-Linares & Robert Liu-Trujillo, *Alejandria Fights Back!/ila lucha de Alejandria!* Uma Krishnaswami, *Book Uncle & Me* Kurusa & Monika Doppert, *The Streets Are Free* Emily Arnold McCully, *The Bobbin Girl* Lindsey H. Metcalf, Keila V. Dawson & Jeanette Bradley (eds.), *No Voice Too Small: Fourteen Young Americans Making History* Innosanto Nagara, *A Is for Activist* Innosanto Nagara, *Oh, the Things We're For!* Kathryn Otoshi, *One* Elinor Batezat Sisulu & Sharon Wilson, *The Day Gogo Went to Vote*

Canonical Texts	Contemporary Texts	Unit Focus	Critical Essential Questions	Sample Supplementary Texts
				<u>Poetry</u> Maya Angelou, "Still I Rise" Mahogany L. Browne, *Woke: A Young Poet's Call to Justice* Allison Adelle Hedge Coke, "America, I Sing You Back" Donte Collins, "What the Dead Know by Heart" Laura Da', "Passive Voice" Ross Gay, "A Small Needful Fact" Martín Espada, "The Republic of Poetry" Langston Hughes, "I Look at the World" Martin Niemöller, "First They Came for the Communists" Naomi Shihab Nye, "Gate A-4" Tino Villanueva, "You, If No One Else" Ella Wheeler Wilcox, "Protest" **<u>Music</u>** Bob Marley, "Get Up Stand Up" Public Enemy, "Fight the Power" Naomi Scott, "Speechless" Buffalo Springfield, "For What It's Worth" Aaron Tippin, "You've Got to Stand for Something" **<u>Art</u>** Arwa Haider, "The Street Art That Expressed the World's Pain" Cynthia Levinson & Evan Turk, *The People's Painter: How Ben Shahn Fought for Justice with Art* Jo Rippon, *The Art of Protest*

Canonical Texts	Contemporary Texts	Unit Focus	Critical Essential Questions	Sample Supplementary Texts
Harper Lee, *To Kill a Mockingbird* Mark Twain, *Adventures of Huckleberry Finn*	Melba Pattillo Beals, *Warriors Don't Cry: A Searing Memoir of the Battle to Integrate Little Rock's Central High* Malorie Blackman, *Noughts & Crosses* Lorene Cary, *Black Ice* Chris Crowe, *Mississippi Trial, 1955* Christopher Paul Curtis, *The Watsons Go to Birmingham—1963* Sharon M. Draper, *Stella by Starlight* Karen Hesse, *Witness* Ibram X. Kendi & Nic Stone, *How to Be a (Young) Antiracist* Sue Monk Kidd, *The Secret Life of Bees* Susan Carol McCarthy, *Lay That Trumpet in Our Hands* Marshall Poe & Ellen Lindner, *Little Rock Nine*	**Combatting Anti-Black Racism**	What is racism? Is our society racist, and if so, how? What is the relationship between racism and power? How can we combat racism?	**Film** *A Civil Action* *Dark Waters* *Erin Brockovich* *The Insider* *Newsies* *The Post* *Resist* *Schindler's List* **Plays** Moisés Kaufman and the Tectonic Theatre Project, *The Laramie Project* Cynthia Mercati, *To See the Stars* **Social Movements** #BlackLivesMatter #MeToo #StopAsianHate **YouTube** US Gymnastic Stars Testify before Congress (various clips) **Short Stories** Kate Chopin, "Desiree's Baby" Lawrence Hill, "So What Are You, Anyway?" Toni Morrison, "Recitatif" **Informational Texts** *The Atlantic*, "Your Stories of Racism" Devan Cole, "Graham Denies Systemic Racism Exists in US and Says 'America's Not a Racist Country'" Nicki Lisa Cole, "Definition of Systemic Racism in Sociology" James Goodman, *Stories of Scottsboro* Tiffany Jewell & Aurelia Durand, *This Book Is Anti-Racist: 20 Lessons on How to Wake Up, Take Action, and Do the Work* Mark Kennedy, "'Speak Up!' *Sesame Street* Tackles Racism in TV Special"

Canonical Texts	Contemporary Texts	Unit Focus	Critical Essential Questions	Sample Supplementary Texts
	Jason Reynolds & Brendan Kiely, *All American Boys* Jason Reynolds & Ibram X. Kendi, *Stamped: Racism, Antiracism, and You* Jewell Parker Rhodes, *Ghost Boys* Nic Stone, *Dear Martin* Mildred D. Taylor, *Roll of Thunder, Hear My Cry* Ibi Zoboi & Yusef Salaam, *Punching the Air*			Martin Luther King Jr., "I Have a Dream" Kyle Korver, "Privileged" Mary Mebane, "The Back of the Bus" Brent Staples, "Black Men and Public Space" **Picture Books** Becky Birtha & Colin Bootman, *Grandmama's Pride* Keila V. Dawson & Alleanna Harris, *Opening the Road: Victor Hugo Green and His Green Book* Judith Bloom Fradin, Dennis Brindell Fradin & Eric Velasquez, *The Price of Freedom: How One Town Stood Up to Slavery* Anastasia Higginbotham, *Not My Idea: A Book about Whiteness* Amy Littlesugar & Floyd Cooper, *Freedom School, Yes!* Duncan Tonatiuh, *Separate Is Never Equal: Sylvia Mendez and Her Family's Fight for Desegregation* Carole Boston Weatherford & Jerome Lagarrigue, *Freedom on the Menu: The Greensboro Sit Ins* Deborah Wiles & Jerome Lagarrigue, *Freedom Summer* Jacqueline Woodson & E. B. Lewis, *The Other Side* **Poetry** Maya Angelou, "Equality" Maya Angelou, "Still I Rise" Nikki Giovanni, "Rosa Parks" Langston Hughes, "Freedom" Langston Hughes, "Freedom's Plow" Langston Hughes, "I, Too"

Canonical Texts	Contemporary Texts	Unit Focus	Critical Essential Questions	Sample Supplementary Texts
				Edna St. Vincent Millay, "Justice Denied in Massachusetts" Dudley Randall, "Ballad of Birmingham" Claudia Rankine, "From Citizen, VI [On the Train the Woman Standing]" **Music** Beyoncé, "Freedom" Black Eyed Peas, "Where Is the Love?" Aretha Franklin, "Think" Ben Harper & Jack Johnson, "With My Own Two Hands" Isley Brothers, "Fight the Power" Bob Marley, "Buffalo Soldier" Outkast, "Rosa Parks" Nina Simone, "Mississippi Goddam" **Art** Nancy Churnin & Felicia Marshall, *Beautiful Shades of Brown: The Art of Laura Wheeler Waring* Telfair Books, *Freedom's March: Photographs of the Civil Rights Movement in Savannah by Frederick C. Baldwin* **Film** *42* *Freedom Writers Glory* *Green Book* *Hairspray* *Harriet* *Hidden Figures* *I Am Not Your Negro* *Loving* *Malcolm X* *Pleasantville* *Race* *Selma* **Plays** Christopher Demos-Brown, *American Son*

Canonical Texts	Contemporary Texts	Unit Focus	Critical Essential Questions	Sample Supplementary Texts
				Rebecca Gilman, *Spinning into Butter* Katori Hall, *The Mountaintop* **Social Movement** #BlackLivesMatter
Ray Bradbury, *Fahrenheit 451* George Orwell, *1984*	Laurie Halse Anderson, *Speak* M. T. Anderson, *Feed* Avi, *Nothing but the Truth* Patricia Forde, *The List* Nat Hentoff, *The Day They Came to Arrest the Book* Kathryn Latsky, *Memoirs of a Bookbat* Lois Lowry, *The Giver* Carolyn Meyer, *Drummers of Jericho* Alan Moore & David Lloyd, *V for Vendetta* Richard Peck, *The Last Safe Place on Earth* Rodman Philbrick, *The Last Book in the Universe* Ayn Rand, *Anthem* M. K. Reed, *Americus* Angie Thomas, *On the Come Up* Scott Westerfeld, *Uglies* Markus Zusak, *The Book Thief*	**Freedom of Thought, Speech, and Expression**	How are freedoms of thought, speech, language, and expression limited? Why might those in power limit freedoms of thought, speech, language, and expression? Should we protect freedoms of thought, speech, language, and expression? And if so, how?	**Short Stories** Ray Bradbury, "Usher II" Luisa Valenzuela, "The Censors" Kurt Vonnegut, "Harrison Bergeron" **Informational Text** Floyd Abrams, "The First Amendment Is the Soul of Our Democracy" aclu.org, "What's Wrong with Public Video Surveillance? Here's 4 Problems" ala.org, "Banned and Challenged Books" Britannica, "Permissible Restrictions on Expression" Virginia Chamlee, "Donald Trump Says He Is Suing Facebook, Twitter, Google over Bans: A Very Beautiful Development" Frederick Douglass, "Learning to Read and Write" history.com, "Edward Snowden Discloses U.S. Government Operations" Mickey Huff & Andy Lee Roth (eds.), *Project Censored's State of the Free Press 2021* Kirk Johnson, "Today's Kids Are, Like, Killing the English Language" Adam Liptak, "Supreme Court Rules for Cheerleader Punished for Vulgar Snapchat Message"

Canonical Texts	Contemporary Texts	Unit Focus	Critical Essential Questions	Sample Supplementary Texts
				Peter Brown, *Mr. Tiger Goes Wild* Paul Buckley & Kate Buckley, *Amy Belligera and the Fireflies* Jacques Goldstyn, *Letters to a Prisoner* Helen Lester & Lynn Munsinger, *Tacky the Penguin* Toni Morrison & Giselle Potter, *The Big Box* **<u>Poetry</u>** Sylvia Chidi, "Freedom Is Walking" Jayne Cortez, "The Oppressionists" Stephen Crane, "Think as I Think" Jeffrey McDaniel, "The Quiet World" Lev Oborin, "From 'Translations in Bare Outline'" **<u>Music</u>** Green Day, "American Idiot" Metallica, "Eye of the Beholder" Muse, "Uprising" Power Quest, "Freedom of Thought" Sorrow, "Illusion of Freedom" 2 Live Crew, "Banned in the USA" **<u>Art</u>** Norman Rockwell, *Freedom of Speech* Hallie Sekoff, "Censored: 10 Artists Who Have Been Persecuted for Their Work" **<u>TV</u>** *Black Mirror*, "Arkangel" *The Twilight Zone*, "Number 12 Looks Just Like You"

Canonical Texts	Contemporary Texts	Unit Focus	Critical Essential Questions	Sample Supplementary Texts
				Films *Citizenfour* *Forbidden Voices* *Good Night, and Good Luck* *Hairspray* *Mediastan* *No Safe Spaces* *Shouting Fire: Stories from the Edge of Free Speech* *Shut Up and Sing* *The Post* **YouTube** John Green, "On the Banning of *Looking for Alaska*"
William Golding, *Lord of the Flies* George Orwell, *Animal Farm* William Shakespeare, *Julius Caesar* William Shakespeare, *Macbeth* William Shakespeare, *Richard III* John Steinbeck, *The Winter of Our Discontent*	Chimamanda Ngozi Adichie, *Purple Hibiscus* Samira Ahmed, *Internment* Margaret Atwood, *The Handmaid's Tale* Jennifer Lynn Barnes, *The Fixer* Rick Bowers, *Spies of Mississippi: The True Story of the Spy Network That Tried to Destroy the Civil Rights Movement* Ally Carter, *All Fall Down* (Embassy Row series) Suzanne Collins, *The Hunger Games* Robert Cormier, *The Chocolate War* Melanie Crowder, *An Uninterrupted View of the Sky* Cory Doctorow, *Little Brother* Sharon M. Draper, *The Battle of Jericho* Lois Duncan, *Killing Mr. Griffin* Ashley Elston, *This Is Our Story* Nancy Farmer, *The House of the Scorpion* Gail Giles, *Shattering Glass* Marie Lu, *Legend*	**Power and Corruption**	Does power lead to corruption?	**Short Stories** Gabriel García Márquez, "One of These Days" Gloria D. Miklowitz, "Confession" Ellen Oh, "The Last Day" Richard Peck, "Priscilla and the Wimps" Saki, "Hermann the Irascible" Henry Slesar, "Examination Day" Hernando Téllez, "Lather and Nothing Else" Will Weaver, "The Photograph" **Informational Texts** John Antonakis, "Does Power Lead to Corruption?" Adam Grant, "Power Doesn't Corrupt. It Just Exposes Who Leaders Really Are" Zoe Christen Jones & Justin Carissimo, "Britney Spears' Conservatorship, Explained" Brian Mann, "Sackler Family Empire Poised to Win Immunity from Opioid Lawsuits" Stanley Milgram, "The Perils of Obedience"

Canonical Texts	Contemporary Texts	Unit Focus	Critical Essential Questions	Sample Supplementary Texts
	Alan Moore & David Lloyd, *V for Vendetta* Carrie Ryan, *Daughter of Deep Silence* Victoria Schwab, *This Savage Song* Todd Strasser, *The Wave* Scott Westerfeld, *Peeps* Ting-xing Ye, *My Name Is Number 4: A True Story from the Cultural Revolution*			Debra A. Miller, *Political Corruption and the Abuse of Power* Elizabeth Rusch, *You Call This Democracy? How to Fix Our Government and Deliver Power to the People* Christopher Shea, "Why Power Corrupts" Kate Shoup, *Corruption in Politics* **Picture Books** Eve Bunting & David Frampton, *Riding the Tiger*

Canonical Texts	Contemporary Texts	Unit Focus	Critical Essential Questions	Sample Supplementary Texts
				Dave Horowitz, *Never Satisfied: The Story of the Stonecutter* Victoria Kann & Elizabeth Kann, *Purplicious* Dr. Seuss, *Yertle the Turtle and Other Stories* David Shannon, *How George Radbourn Saved Baseball* Olivier Tallec, *Louis I, King of the Sheep* Stanley Tookie Williams & Barbara Cottman Becnel, *Gangs and the Abuse of Power* **<u>Poetry</u>** Emily Dickinson, "I Took Power in My Hand" Francis Duggan, "Those Who Abuse Their Power" Francis Duggan, "To Have Power over Others" Lonnie Hicks, "All Power" Robinson Jeffers, "Be Angry at the Sun" George MacDonald, "Power" Carl Sandburg, "The Government" Percy Bysshe Shelley, "Ozymandias" S. D. Tiwari, "Power of Corruption" **<u>Music</u>** The Alarm, "Corridors of Power" DBC, "Power and Corruption" Billie Eilish, "Your Power" Rush, "The Trees" Suzanne Vega, "The Queen and the Soldier" **<u>Film</u>** *All the King's Men* *All the President's Men* *Chinatown* *Dark Money* *Enron: The Smartest Guys in the Room* *A Few Good Men*

Canonical Texts	Contemporary Texts	Unit Focus	Critical Essential Questions	Sample Supplementary Texts
				The Firm *The Last King of Scotland* *The Lord of the Rings: The Fellowship of the Ring* *Michael Clayton* *Point of Order!* *The Social Network* *The Stanford Prison Experiment*
Ray Bradbury, *Farhenheit 451* Joseph Conrad, *Nostromo* Charles Dickens, *A Tale of Two Cities* Victor Hugo, *Les Miserables* Victor Hugo, *Ninety-Three* Aldous Huxley, *Brave New World* Baroness Orczy, *The Scarlet Pimpernel* George Orwell, *Animal Farm* George Orwell, *1984* Thomas Paine, *Common Sense, The Rights of Man, and Other Essential Writings of Thomas Paine* William Shakespeare, *Romeo and Juliet* Sophocles, *Antigone*	Frank Abe, Tamiko Nimura & Ross Ishikawa, *We Hereby Refuse: Japanese American Resistance to Wartime Incarceration* Elliot Ackerman, *Green on Blue* Samira Ahmed, *Internment* Laurie Halse Anderson, *Chains: The Seeds of America* Margaret Atwood, *The Handmaid's Tale* Victoria Aveyard, *Red Queen* Avi, *Nothing but the Truth* Ingrid Betancourt, *The Blue Line* Suzanne Collins, *The Hunger Games* Ying Chang Compestine, *Revolution Is Not a Dinner Party* Ally Condie, *Matched* Robert Cormier, *The Chocolate War* Assia Djebar, *Children of the New World: A Novel of the Algerian War* Cory Doctorow, *Little Brother* Sharon M. Draper, *The Battle of Jericho* Margaret Peterson Haddix, *Among the Hidden* Ira Levin, *This Perfect Day* Lois Lowry, *The Giver* Gemma Malley, *The Declaration*	**Rebellion, Revolution, and Reform**	What constitutes a rebellion and revolution? How and why do we rebel and revolt? Can rebellion and revolution be justified? What are the consequences of rebellion and/or revolution?	**Short Stories** Ray Bradbury, "Usher II" Philip K. Dick, "Minority Report" Henry Dumas, "Riot or Revolt" Harlan Ellison, "Repent, Harlequin! Said the Ticktockman" Shirley Jackson, "The Lottery" N. K. Jemisin, "The Ones Who Stay and Fight" Kurt Vonnegut, "Harrison Bergeron" **Informational Texts** "The Declaration of Independence" Michael Brendan Dougherty, "Anger Is Justified, Riots Never Are" Douglas R. Egerton, "Abolitionist or Terrorist?" Alan Feuer, "How the Capitol Riot Suspects Are Challenging the Charges" history.com, Malcolm X history.com, Mohandas Gandhi Martin Luther King Jr., "I Have a Dream" Michele Langevine Leiby, "Malala Yousafzai: From a Schoolgirl to a Nobel Peace Prize Winner" Philip V. McHarris, "The George Floyd Protests Are a Rebellion against an Unjust System"

Canonical Texts	Contemporary Texts	Unit Focus	Critical Essential Questions	Sample Supplementary Texts
	Christopher Metzger, *Silent Rebellion* Marissa Meyer, *Cinder* Alan Moore & David Lloyd, *V for Vendetta* Ali Nujood, *I Am Nujood, Age 10 and Divorced* Robert C. O'Brien, *Z for Zachariah* Lauren Oliver, *Delirium* Arushi Raina, *When Morning Comes* Ayn Rand, *Anthem* Veronica Roth, *Divergent* Marjane Satrapi, *Persepolis: The Story of a Childhood* Rafik Schami, *A Hand Full of Stars* Neal Shusterman, *Unwind* Meagan Spooner, *Skylark* Todd Strasser, *The Wave* Sabaa Tahir, *An Ember in the Ashes* Brian K. Vaughan, *Runaways, Vol. 1: Pride and Joy* Scott Westerfeld, *Uglies* Suzanne Weyn, *The Bar Code Tattoo* Malala Yousafzai, *I Am Malala: How One Girl Stood Up for Education and Changed the World*			Stanley Milgram, "The Perils of Obedience" Henry David Thoreau, "Civil Disobedience" Robert F. Worth, "Tiny Voices Defy Child Marriage in Yemen" **Picture Books** Eve Bunting, *Terrible Things: An Allegory of the Holocaust* Doreen Cronin & Betsy Lewin, *Click, Clack, Moo: Cows That Type* Carmen Agra Deedy & Eugene Yelchin, *The Rooster Who Would Not Be Quiet!* Ariel Dorfman & Chris Riddell, *The Rabbits' Rebellion* Toni Morrison & Giselle Potter, *The Big Box* Maurice Sendak, *Where the Wild Things Are* **Poetry** Maya Angelou, "Caged Bird" Stephen Crane, "Think As I Think" Kwame Dawes, "Creation Rebel" Mark Eisner & Tina Escaja (eds.), *Resistencia: Poems of Protest and Revolution* Nikki Giovanni, "Rosa Parks" Nathalie Handal, "Ways of Rebelling" Langston Hughes, "I Look at the World" Langston Hughes, "I, Too" Philip Levine, "They Feed the Lion" Adrienne Rich, "What Kind of Times Are These" Tupac Shakur, "The Rose That Grew from Concrete" Percy Bysshe Shelley, "A Song: 'Men of England'"

Canonical Texts	Contemporary Texts	Unit Focus	Critical Essential Questions	Sample Supplementary Texts
				Tino Villanueva, "You, If No One Else" **Music** The Beatles, "Revolution 1" Bob Dylan, "The Times They Are a-Changing" Linkin Park, "Rebellion" Lockdown, "Thrice" Bob Marley, "Get Up, Stand Up" Lin-Manuel Miranda, "My Shot" Muse, "Uprising" Phil Ochs, "I Ain't Marching Anymore" Oingo Boingo, "Perfect System" One Voice HK, "One Voice" Public Enemy, "Fight the Power" Britney Spears, "Rebellion" Taylor Swift, "Change" U2, "Sunday Bloody Sunday" **Art** Christian Hundertmark, The Art of Rebellion (series) Josh MacPhee {ed.), *Celebrate People's History! The Poster Book of Resistance and Revolution* **Photography** David Aretha, *The Story of the Civil Rights March on Washington for Jobs and Freedom in Photographs* Telfair Books, *Freedom's March: Photographs of the Civil Rights Movement in Savannah by Frederick C. Baldwin* **Dance** YouTube, *Dance Rebels: A Story of Modern Dance* **Film** *Che Part I: The Argentine* and *Che Part II: Guerrilla*

Canonical Texts	Contemporary Texts	Unit Focus	Critical Essential Questions	Sample Supplementary Texts
Nathaniel Hawthorne, *The Scarlet Letter* Arthur Miller, *The Crucible*	Randa Abdel-Fattah, *Does My Head Look Big in This?* Randa Abdel-Fattah, *The Lines We Cross* Laurie Halse Anderson, *Speak* Jay Asher, *Thirteen Reasons Why* Laura Bates, *The Burning* L. M. Elliott, *Suspect Red* Nancy Farmer, *The House of the Scorpion* Sharon Flake, *The Skin I'm In* Jeanne Wakatsuki Houston & James D. Houston, *Farewell to Manzanar* Katherine Howe, *Conversion* Kim Johnson, *This Is My America* Sabrina Jones & Marc Mauer, *Race to Incarcerate: A Graphic Retelling* Hillary Jordan, *When She Woke* Dick Lehr, *Trell: Nothing but the Truth* Adriana Mather, *How to Hang a Witch* Denene Millner & Mitzi Miller, *Hotlanta* (Book 1) Walter Dean Myers, *Monster* James Braxton Peterson, *Prison Industrial Complex for Beginners* Celia Rees, *Witch Child* Laura Ruby, *Good Girls*	**Persecution**	How and why do we persecute others? In what ways can we act on behalf of those suffering from unjust persecution?	*Les Misérables* *Malcolm X* *Mandela: Long Walk to Freedom* *The Matrix* *The Patriot* *Red Dawn* *Rogue One: A Star Wars Story* *V for Vendetta* **Short Stories** Nathaniel Hawthorne, "The Birth-Mark" Nathaniel Hawthorne, "Young Goodman Brown" Guy de Maupassant, "The Piece of String" Flannery O'Connor, "Good County People" James Thurber, "The Very Proper Gander" **Informational Texts** Radley Balko, "There's Overwhelming Evidence That the Criminal Justice System Is Racist: Here's the Proof" Deborah Ellis, *My Story Starts Here: Voices of Young Offenders* Aisha Harris, "The Central Park Five: 'We Were Just Baby Boys'" Heather MacDonald, "The Myth of Systemic Police Racism" Arthur Miller, "Are You Now or Were You Ever" David Scharfenberg, "County Ad Puts Spotlight on Parents Who Owe Child Support" Bryan Stevenson, *Just Mercy: A Story of Justice and Redemption* (Adapted for Young Adults) Harry Truman, Loyalty Order, Executive Order 9835 Mark Twain, "Disgraceful Persecution of a Boy"

Canonical Texts	Contemporary Texts	Unit Focus	Critical Essential Questions	Sample Supplementary Texts
	Dashka Slater, *The 57 Bus: A True Story of Two Teenagers and the Crime That Changed Their Lives* Nic Stone, *Dear Justyce* Nic Stone, *Dear Martin* George Takei, Justin Eisinger, Steven Scott, & Harmony Becker, *They Called Us Enemy* Sara Zarr, *Story of a Girl* Ibi Zoboi & Yusef Salaam, *Punching the Air*			**Picture Books** Eve Bunting, *Terrible Things: An Allegory of the Holocaust* Karen Gedig Burnett, *If the World Were Blind . . .: A Book about Judgment and Prejudice* Miriam Nerlove, *Flowers on the Wall* **Poetry** Maya Angelou, "Still I Rise" Margaret Atwood, "Half Hanged Mary" Langston Hughes, "Ballad of the Landlord" Langston Hughes, "Still Here" Harryette Mullen, "We Are Not Responsible" Martin Niemöller, "First They Came for the Socialists" Adrienne Rich, "What Kinds of Times Are These" **Music** Five Man Electric Band, "Signs" Billy Joel, "We Didn't Start the Fire" Bob Marley, "Judge Not" Misfits, "Witch Hunt" Rush, "Witch Hunt" Sly and the Family Stone, "Everyday People" The Smiths, "Barbarism Begins at Home" Bruce Springsteen, "Devils & Dust" **Art** Kayla Webley, "Top 10 Persecuted Artists" **Film** *Brian Banks* *The Central Park Five* *Footloose* *Free Meek* *Good Night, and Good Luck* *If Beale Street Could Talk*

Canonical Texts	Contemporary Texts	Unit Focus	Critical Essential Questions	Sample Supplementary Texts
				Just Mercy *The Learning Tree* *The Matthew Shepard Story* *Miracle in Cell No. 7* *The Shawshank Redemption* *13th* *TIME: The Kalief Browder Story* *12 Angry Men* *When They See Us* **Play** Dominique Morisseau, *Pipeline* **YouTube** "Dog Shaming Highlights" Monthy Python, "She's a Witch!"
F. Scott Fitzgerald, *The Great Gatsby* Lorraine Hansberry, *A Raisin in the Sun* Arthur Miller, *Death of a Salesman* John Steinbeck, *The Grapes of Wrath* John Steinbeck, *Of Mice and Men*	Sherman Alexie, *The Absolutely True Diary of a Part-Time Indian* Julissa Arce, *Someone Like Me: How One Undocumented Girl Fought for Her American Dream* Ann Bausum, *Denied, Detained, Deported: Stories from the Dark Side of American Immigration* Sara Benincasa, *Great* Melissa de la Cruz, *Some Thing in Between* Sampson Davis, George Jenkins, and Rameck Hunt, *The Pact* Malaka Gharib, *I Was Their American Dream: A Graphic Memoir* Patrick Jones, *Bridge* An Na, *A Step from Heaven* Pam Muñoz Ryan, *Esperanza Rising* Erika L. Sánchez, *I Am Not Your Perfect Mexican Daughter* Anne Schraff, *Second Chances* Angie Thomas, *The Hate U Give*	**American Dream**	What is the American Dream? How does a diverse America affect the stereotypical American Dream? Is the American Dream equally accessible? How can we help each other reach our American Dreams?	**Short Stories** F. Scott Fitzgerald, "Winter Dreams" O. Henry, "Mammon and the Archer" Francisco Jiménez, *The Circuit: Stories from the Life of a Migrant Child* Isaac Bashevis Singer, "The Son from America" Amy Tan, "Two Kinds" **Informational Texts** Gale Student Resources in Context, "How the American Dream Has Changed over Time" Kyle Korver, "Privileged" Steve Large, "UC Davis Economics Professor: There Is No American Dream" Marie Myung-Ok Lee, "I Was an 'Anchor Baby'" Michael Lewis, "The Ballad of Big Mike" Eric Liu, *A Chinaman's Chance: One Family's Journey and the Chinese American Dream* Mary Beth McLaughlin, "Lifelong Dreamer—Vietnam Boat Person"

Canonical Texts	Contemporary Texts	Unit Focus	Critical Essential Questions	Sample Supplementary Texts
	Helen Thorpe, *The Newcomers: Finding Refuge, Friendship, and Hope in an American Classroom* Jeannette Walls, *The Glass Castle: A Memoir* Nicola Yoon, *The Sun Is Also a Star* Ibi Zoboi, *American Street*			Mathew O'Brien, "The Great Gatsby Curve: Why It's So Hard for the Poor to Get Ahead" Linda Barrett Osborne, *This Land Is Our Land: A History of American Immigration* Dan Rather, "They Live the Dream" Robert J. Shiller, "The Transformation of the 'American Dream'" Al Tompkins, "What Is the American Dream in 2020 . . . If There Is One?" Anzia Yezierska, "America and I" Mohamed Younis, "Most Americans See American Dream as Achievable" **<u>Picture Books</u>** Linda Jacobs Altman & Enrique O. Sanchez, *Amelia's Road* Avi & C. B. Mordan, *Silent Movie* Samad Behrangi & Farshid Mesghali, *The Little Black Fish* René Colato Laínez and Joe Cepeda, *From North to South* Fiona McEntee & Srimalie Bassani, *Our American Dream* Walter Dean Myers & Christopher Myers, *We Are America: A Tribute from the Heart* Duncan Tonatiuh, *Undocumented: A Worker's Fight* Barry Wittenstein, Kristen Howdeshell & Kevin Howdeshell, *Oscar's American Dream* Dan Yaccarino, *All the Way to America: The Story of a Big Italian Family and a Little Shovel*

Canonical Texts	Contemporary Texts	Unit Focus	Critical Essential Questions	Sample Supplementary Texts
				<u>Poetry</u> Jack Agüeros, "Alan, American Dreamer" Allen Ginsberg, "America" Juan Felipe Herrera, "Every Day We Get More Illegal" Langston Hughes, "A Dream Deferred" Langston Hughes, "Let America Be America Again" Langston Hughes, "Mother to Son" Tato Laviera, "lady liberty" Emma Lazarus, "The New Colossus" Blas Manuel de Luna, "Bent to the Earth" Claude McKay, "America" Pat Mora, "Legal Alien" Ricardo Sánchez, "I Yearn" Tupac Shakur, "The Rose That Grew from Concrete" Walt Whitman, "I Hear America Singing" **<u>Music</u>** David Bowie. "Young Americans" James Brown, "America Is My Home, Part I" James Brown, "Living in America" Miley Cyrus, "The Climb" Neil Diamond, "America" Childish Gambino, "This Is America" Michael Jackson, "They Don't Care about Us" Lorde, "Royals" Madonna, "American Life" John Mellencamp, "Pink Houses" The Notorious B.I.G. "Juicy"

Canonical Texts	Contemporary Texts	Unit Focus	Critical Essential Questions	Sample Supplementary Texts
				Art Thomas Hart Benton, "America Today" Tiago Hoisel, "The American Dream" Dorothea Lange, "Migrant Mother" Norman Rockwell, "Freedom from Want" Andy Warhol, *Campbell's Soup Cans* Grant Wood, "American Gothic" **TV/Film** *An American Tail* *The Blind Side* *Forrest Gump* *Hoop Dreams* *Minari* *Pleasantville* *The Pursuit of Happyness* **Play** Lin-Manuel Miranda, *Hamilton* Tennessee Williams, *A Streetcar Named Desire* **YouTube** John Green, "Is the American Dream Real?" **TikTok** "My Life Be Like" **Instagram** #VanLife
Anne Frank, *The Diary of a Young Girl* Eli Weisel, *Night*	Adam Bagdasarian, *Forgotten Fire* Ishmael Beah, *A Long Way Gone: Memoirs of a Boy Soldier* Sharon Cameron, *The Light in Hidden Places* Élisabeth Combres, *Broken Memory: A Novel of Rwanda* Brian Crawford, *The Weaver's Scar: For Our Rwanda* John Bul Dau & Martha Arual Akech, *Lost Boy, Lost Girl: Escaping Civil War in Sudan* Benson Deng, Alephonsion	**Genocide**	Why and how does genocide occur? What actions can be taken to prevent genocide?	**Multiple Genres** Jean E. Brown, Elaine C. Stephens & Janet E. Rubin (eds.), *Images from the Holocaust: A Literature Anthology* Albert H. Friedlander (ed.), *Out of the Whirlwind: A Reader of Holocaust Literature* Lawrence L. Langer (ed.), *Art from the Ashes: A Holocaust Anthology* Milton Teichman & Sharon Leder (eds.), *Truth and Lamentation: Stories and Poems on the Holocaust*

Canonical Texts	Contemporary Texts	Unit Focus	Critical Essential Questions	Sample Supplementary Texts
	Deng & Benjamin Ajak, *They Poured Fire on Us from the Sky: The True Story of Three Lost Boys from Sudan* Sharon Dogar, *Annexed* Sharon M. Draper, *Copper Sun* Steven Galloway, *The Cellist of Sarajevo* Alan Gratz, *Prisoner B-3087* Monica Hesse, *Girl in the Blue Coat* Hanna Jansen, *Over a Thousand Hills I Walk with You* Elizabeth Laird, *Kiss the Dust* Patricia McCormick, *Never Fall Down* Ben Mikaelsen, *Tree Girl* Irene Gut Opdyke, *In My Hands: Memories of a Holocaust Rescuer* Linda Sue Park, *A Long Walk to Water* Amra Sabic-El-Rayess, *The Cat I Never Named: A True Story of Love, War, and Survival* Ruta Sepetys, *Between Shades of Gray* Marsha Forchuk Skrypuch, *Nobody's Child* Art Spiegelman, *Maus: A Survivor's Tale* J. P. Stassen, *Deogratias: A Tale of Rwanda* Loung Ung, *First They Killed My Father: A Daughter of Cambodia Remembers* Sandra Uwiringiyimana, *How Dare the Sun Rise: Memoirs of a War Child* Dana Walrath, *Like Water on a Stone* Sylvia Whitman, *The Milk of Birds* Markus Zusak, *The Book Thief*			**Short Stories** Linda Schermer Raphael & Marc Lee Raphael, *When Night Fell: An Anthology of Holocaust Short Stories* **Informational Texts** Dee Brown, *Bury My Heart at Wounded Knee: An Indian History of the American West* Thomas Fuller & Julia Wallace, "2 Khmer Rouge Leaders Are Convicted in Cambodia" General Assembly of the United Nations, "Convention on the Prevention and Punishment of the Crime of Genocide" Suyin Haynes, "They Were Orphaned by the Rwandan Genocide: 25 Years Later, They're Interviewing the Perpetrators" Aida Kouyoumjian, *Between the Two Rivers: A Story of the Armenian Genocide* Sarah Parvini, Melissa Gomez & Alex Wigglesworth, "Armenian American Activists Welcome U.S. Recognition of Genocide; Say Fight Isn't Over" Selena Salihovic, "Selena's Story: A Survivor of the Bosnian Genocide" United States Holocaust Memorial Museum, Holocaust-era Diaries United States Holocaust Memorial Museum, "An Introduction to the Holocaust" United States Holocaust Memorial Museum, "Iraq: Our Generation Is Gone"

Canonical Texts	Contemporary Texts	Unit Focus	Critical Essential Questions	Sample Supplementary Texts
				Picture Books Chana Byers Abells, *The Children We Remember* Alvin Abram & Judy Nora Willemsma, *Why, Zaida?* Eve Bunting, *Terrible Things: An Allegory of the Holocaust* Mem Fox & Nicholas Wilton, *Feathers and Fools* Jeff Gottesfeld & Peter McCarty, *The Tree in the Courtyard: Looking through Anne Frank's Window* Patricia Polacco, *The Butterfly* Patricia Polacco, *January's Sparrow* Icy Smith & Sopaul Nhem, *Half Spoon of Rice: A Survival Story of the Cambodian Genocide* Ruth Vander Zee & Roberto Innocenti, *Erika's Story* Mary Williams & R. Gregory Christie, *Brothers in Hope: The Story of the Lost Boys of Sudan* Meg Wiviott & Josée Bisaillon, *Benno and the Night of Broken Glass* Jane Yolen & David Shannon, *Encounter* **Poetry** Martin Niemöller, "First They Came for the Communists" Hilda Schiff (ed.), *Holocaust Poetry* Hana Volavková (ed.), *I Never Saw Another Butterfly: Children's Drawings and Poems from Terezín Concentration Camp, 1942–1944* **Music** Indigo Girls, "This Train" Bob Marley, "Redemption Song" Midnight Oil, "Beds Are Burning"

Canonical Texts	Contemporary Texts	Unit Focus	Critical Essential Questions	Sample Supplementary Texts
				R.E.M., "The Flowers of Guatemala" Buffy Sainte-Marie, "My Country 'Tis of Thy People You're Dying" System of a Down, "P.L.U.C.K." United States Holocaust Memorial Museum, "Music of the Holocaust" U2, "Bullet the Blue Sky" Neil Young, "Cortez the Killer" **Art** Max D. Standley, "Trail of Tears" **Photography** camerakids.photos, Through the Eyes of Children United States Holocaust Memorial Museum, Photo Archives **Film** *Aghet: A Genocide* *Bury My Heart at Wounded Knee* *Enemies of the People* *The Good Lie* (2014) *The Holocaust: History and Memory* (A Virtual Tour) (ushmm.org) *Hotel Rwanda* *The Killing Fields* *The Last Survivor* (2010) *Letters from Kurdistan* *Lost Boys of Sudan* *The Path to Nazi Genocide* (ushmm.org) *We Shall Remain: America through Native Eyes* **Podcast** United States Holocaust Memorial Museum, *First Person: Conversations with Holocaust Survivors*

Canonical Texts	Contemporary Texts	Unit Focus	Critical Essential Questions	Sample Supplementary Texts
Victor Hugo, *The Hunchback of Notre Dame* John Steinbeck, *Of Mice and Men*	S. K. Ali, *Love from A to Z* Josh Berk, *The Dark Days of Hamburger Halpin* Priscilla Cummings, *Blindsided* Justina Chen, *Lovely, Dark, and Deep* Marci Lyn Curtis, *The One Thing* Sharon M. Draper, *Out of My Mind* Corinne Duyvis, *On the Edge of Gone* Sharon G. Flake, *Pinned* Lucy Frank, *Two Girls Staring at the Ceiling* Natasha Friend, *How We Roll* Jonathan Friesen, *Jerk, California* Helen Frost, *All He Knew* Yuki Fumino, *I Hear the Sunspot* Whitney Gardner, *You're Welcome, Universe* Alison Gervais, *The Silence between Us* Gail Giles, *Girls Like Us* John Green, *The Fault in Our Stars* Mark Haddon, *The Curious Incident of the Dog in the Night-Time* April Henry, *Girl, Stolen* Mariatu Kamara, *The Bite of the Mango* Kody Keplinger, *Run* Michelle Krys, *Dead Girls Society* Nick Lake, *There Will Be Lies* Mackenzi Lee, *The Gentleman's Guide to Vice and Virtue* Eric Lindstrom, *Not If I See You First* Sonya Mukherjee, *Gemini* Marieke Nijkamp, *The Oracle Code* R. J. Palacio, *Wonder*	**Physical and Mental Ableism**	What are kinds of physical and mental challenges? How are people with physical and mental challenges defying stereotypes? What is the relationship between power and disability? What are ways we can advocate for people who have physical and mental challenges?	**<u>Short Stories</u>** Octavia E. Butler, "Speech Sounds" Raymond Carver, "Cathedral" Joanne Greenberg, "And Sarah Laughed" James Hurst, "The Scarlet Ibis" MacKinlay Kantor, "A Man Who Had No Eyes" Ken Liu, "The Plague" Meg Mingus, "Hollow" Elinor Nash, "Ghost Boy" Marieke Nijkamp, (ed.), *Unbroken: 13 Stories Starring Disabled Teens* **<u>Informational Texts</u>** Agence France-Presse, "Myanmar Teen Soccer Star Defies the Odds" Edward C. Baig, "Video Games Are a 'Great Equalizer' for People with Disabilities" Shane Burcaw, *Laughing At My Nightmare* Jessica Chiu, "On YouTube, People with Disabilities Create Content to Show and Normalize Their Experiences" Judith Heumann, *Being Heumann: An Unrepentant Memoir of a Disability Rights Activist* Peri Meldon, "Disability History: The Disability Rights Movement" Kim E. Nielsen, *A Disability History of the United States* Michael Part, *The Greta Thunberg Story: Being Different Is a Superpower* Amy Sequenzia & Elizabeth J. Grace (eds.), *Typed Words Loud Voices* Rodman Philbrick, *Freak the Mighty*

Canonical Texts	Contemporary Texts	Unit Focus	Critical Essential Questions	Sample Supplementary Texts
	Rebecca Podos, *Like Water* NoNieqa Ramos, *The Disturbed Girl's Dictionary* Marcus Sedgwick, *She Is Not Invisible* Francisco X. Stork, *Marcelo in the Real World* Krystal Sutherland, *Our Chemical Hearts* Leah Thomas, *Because You'll Never Meet Me* Wendelin Van Draanen, *The Running Dream* Padma Venkatraman, *A Time to Dance* Julia Walton, *Words on Bathroom Walls* Jen Wilde, *Queens of Geek* Jacquelyn Woodson, *Hush*			Theresa Vargas, "This College Sophomore Wants to Change How We Talk about Disabilities" **Picture Books** Linda Jacobs Altman & Larry Johnson, *Singing with Momma Lou* Menena Cottin & Rosana Faría, *The Black Book of Colors* Kirsten DeBear & Laura Dwight, *Be Quiet, Marina!* Zetta Elliott & Purple Wong, *Benny Doesn't Like to Be Hugged* Juan Felipe Herrera & Ernesto Cuevas Jr., *Featherless: Desplumado* Helen Lester & Lynn Munsinger, *Tacky the Penguin* Julia Finley Mosca & Daniel Rieley, *The Girl Who Thought in Pictures: The Story of Dr. Temple Grandin* Patricia Polacco, *Thank You, Mr. Falker* Pete Seeger, Paul Dubois Jacobs & R. Gregory Christie, *The Deaf Musicians* Simran Jeet Singh & Baljinder Kaur, *Fauja Singh Keeps Going: The True Story of the Oldest Person to Ever Run a Marathon* Sonia Sotomayor & Rafael López, *Just Ask! Be Different, Be Brave, Be You* Laurie Ann Thompson & Sean Qualls, *Emmanuel's Dream: The True Story of Emmanual Ofosu Yeboah* **Poetry** Sheila Black (ed.), *Beauty Is a Verb: The New Poetry of Disability*

Canonical Texts	Contemporary Texts	Unit Focus	Critical Essential Questions	Sample Supplementary Texts
				John Lee Clark, "A DeafBlind Poet" John Lee Clark, "The Rebuttal" Linda Cronin "Flash Essay on: Beauty and the Beholder" Barbara Crooker, "45s, LPs" Zoeglossia Fellows (ed.), *We Are Not Your Metaphor: A Disability Poetry Anthology* Meg Day, "Deaf Erasure of the Gospel According to the TSA Agent at Atlanta International" Jim Ferris, "Poems with Disabilities" Ona Gritz, "Passing" Marie Kane, "Radio Interview" Michael Morrell, "Instructions for Hugging the Dwarf Goodbye at the Writer's Conference" Stuart Sanderson, "Maddening" Jillian Weise, "I Want Your Fax" **<u>Music</u>** Alessia Cara, "Scars to Your Beautiful" Jane Field, *The Fishing Is Free* Sean Forbes, "Watch These Hands" Jessie J, "Who You Are" Keala Settle, "This Is Me" Staff Benda Bilili, "Mwana" **<u>Podcast</u>** Leroy F. Moore (Founder of Krip-Hop Nation) **<u>Film</u>** *A Brilliant Young Mind* *Chemical Hearts* *Crip Camp* *The Greatest Showman* *I Am Sam* *Life, Animated*

Canonical Texts	Contemporary Texts	Unit Focus	Critical Essential Questions	Sample Supplementary Texts
				Mozart and the Whale *The Other Sister* *Soul Surfer* *Swim Team* (2016) *The Upside* *Wonder* *Words on Bathroom Walls* **Play** Andrew Hinderaker, *Colossal* **Social Movement** Choose Kind
Louisa May Alcott, *Little Women* Jane Austen, *Emma* Kate Chopin, *The Awakening* William Golding, *Lord of the Flies* Henrik Ibsen, *A Doll's House* Henry James, *The Portrait of a Lady* William Shakespeare, *Taming of the Shrew* William Shakespeare, *Twelfth Night* Sophocles, *Antigone* Virginia Woolf, *A Room of One's Own*	Fred Aceves, *The New David Espinoza* Naomi Alderman, *The Power* Margaret Atwood, *The Handmaid's Tale* Libba Bray, *Beauty Queens* Candace Bushnell & Katie Cotugno, *Rules for Being a Girl* Emily M. Danforth, *The Miseducation of Cameron Post* April Daniels, *Dreadnought* Alex Flinn, *Fade to Black* Camryn Garrett, *Full Disclosure* Lamar Giles, *Not So Pure and Simple* M-E. Girard, *Girl Mans Up* John Green & David Levithan, *Will Grayson, Will Grayson* I. W. Gregorio, *None of the Above* A. M. Homes, *Jack* Brian Katcher, *Almost Perfect* Sabina Khan, *Love & Lies of Rukhsana Ali* Sophie LaBelle, *Ciel* Mackenzi Lee, *The Lady's Guide to Petticoats and Piracy* Jennifer Mathieu, *Moxie* Tehlor Kay Mejia, *We Set the Dark on Fire*	**Gender and Attraction**	What are gender stereotypes? How are stereotypes about gender and attraction constructed and perpetuated? Does gender play a role in attraction? If so, how? How are people challenging traditional/stereotypical notions of gender and attraction?	**Short Stories** Marion Dane Bauer (ed.), *Am I Blue: Coming Out from the Silence* Kate Chopin, "The Story of an Hour" Charlotte Perkins Gilman, "The Yellow Wallpaper" Ernest Hemingway, "The Short Happy Life of Francis Macomber" Doris Lessing, "To Room Nineteen" Sirius Métier (ed.), *To Be Men: Stories Celebrating Masculinity* Alice Munro, "Boys and Girls" Julie Anne Peters, *Grl2grl* Andrea Davis Pinkney, "Building Bridges" Bennett Singer (ed.), *Growing Up Gay/Lesbian: A Literary Anthology* **Informational Texts** Judy Brady, "I Want a Wife" Katie Cappiello (ed.), *Now That We're Men: A Play and True Life Accounts of Boys, Sex & Power* Melissa de la Cruz (ed.), *Because I Was a Girl: True Stories for Girls of All Ages* Kelly Huegel, *GLBTQ: The Survival Guide for Gay, Lesbian, Bisexual, Transgender, and Questioning Teens*

Canonical Texts	Contemporary Texts	Unit Focus	Critical Essential Questions	Sample Supplementary Texts
	Louise O'Neill, *Only Ever Yours* Sonia Patel, *Jaaya and Rasa: A Love Story* Julie Anne Peters, *Keeping You a Secret* Julie Anne Peters, *Luna* Isabel Quintero, *Gabi, A Girl in Pieces* Gabby Rivera, *Juliet Takes a Breath* Meredith Russo, *If I Was Your Girl* Alex Sanchez, *Bait* Alex Sanchez, *Boyfriends with Girlfriends* Alex Sanchez, *Rainbow Boys* Pat Schmatz, *Lizard Radio* Lisa Williamson, *The Art of Being Normal* G. Willow Wilson, Ms. Marvel series Jacqueline Woodson, *From the Notebooks of Melanin Sun*			Kelly Jensen (ed.), *Here We Are: Feminism for the Real World* Mariam Khan (ed.), *It's Not about the Burqa: Muslim Women on Faith, Feminism, Sexuality and Race* Susan Kuklin, *Beyond Magenta: Transgender Teens Speak Out* Belinda Luscombe, "Kids Believe Gender Stereotypes by Age 10, Global Study Finds" Michael Mascolo, "Time to Move beyond 'Gender Is Socially Constructed'" David M. Mayer, "How Men Get Penalized for Straying from Masculine Norms" Alleen Pace Nilsen, "Sexism in English: Embodiment and Language" Robyn Ryle, *She/He/They/Me: For the Sisters, Misters, and Binary Resisters* Lindsey Tanner, "Not Just Boy and Girl; More Teens Identify as Transgender" John Updike, "The Disposable Rocket" Alok Vaid-Menon, *Beyond the Gender Binary* Mary Wollstonecraft, *A Vindication of the Rights of Woman* Virginia Woolf, "Shakespeare's Sister" **Picture Books** Anthony Browne, *Piggybook* Eric Carle, *Mister Seahorse* Stacy B. Davids & Rachel Balsaitis, *Annie's Plaid Shirt* Tomie dePaola, *Oliver Button Is a Sissy* Julia Donaldson & Axel Scheffler, *Zog*

Canonical Texts	Contemporary Texts	Unit Focus	Critical Essential Questions	Sample Supplementary Texts
				Mary Hoffman & Caroline Binch, *Amazing Grace* Munro Leaf & Robert Lawson, *The Story of Ferdinand* Robert Munsch & Michael Martchenko, *The Paper Bag Princess* Leslea Newman, *Sparkle Boy* Vivek Shraya & Rajni Perera, *The Boy and the Bindi* Theresa Thorn & Noah Grigni, *It Feels Good to Be Yourself: A Book about Gender Identity* **<u>Poetry</u>** A. R. Ammons, "Working with Tools" Maya Angelou, "Woman Work" Cameron Awkward-Rich, "Cento between the Ending and the End" Jari Bradley, "Unruly" Gwendolyn Brooks, "Bronzeville Man with a Belt in the Back" Lucille Clifton, "Homage to My Hips" Lucille Clifton, "The Kind of Man He Is" Lucille Clifton, "My Daddy's Fingers Move among the Couplers" Lucille Clifton, "My Mama Moved among the Days" Lucille Clifton, "Sisters" Regie Cabico, "A Queerification" Rita Dove, "Party Dress for a First Born" Nikki Giovanni, "Beautiful Black Men" Donald Justice, "The Missing Person" Carolyn Kizer, "Pro Femina"

Canonical Texts	Contemporary Texts	Unit Focus	Critical Essential Questions	Sample Supplementary Texts
				Marge Piercy, "Barbie Doll" Theodore Roethke, "My Papa's Waltz" W. D. Snodgrass, "Viewing the Body" **<u>Music</u>** Big Sean, "One Man Can Change the World" Blur, "Girls & Boys" Craig Campbell, "Family Man" Harry Chapin, "Cat's in the Cradle" The Cure, "Boys Don't Cry" Hazel Dickens, "The Rebel Girl" Ani DiFranco, "Not a Pretty Girl" Peter Gabriel & Youssou N'Dour, "Shaking the Tree" Michael Jackson, "Man in the Mirror" The Killers, "The Man" Lady Gaga, "Born This Way" No Doubt, "Just a Girl" Helen Reddy, "I Am Woman" Tupac Shakur, "Keep Ya Head Up" Dar Williams, "When I Was a Boy" **<u>Art</u>** Google Arts & Culture, "The Feminist Artists Whose Work You Need to Know" Charlotte Jansen, "How Photographers Have Challenged What Masculinity Looks Like" nbcnews.com, "12 Queer Artists Whose Work Is Making Us Pay Attention" **<u>Film</u>** *Bend It Like Beckham* *Dangal*

Canonical Texts	Contemporary Texts	Unit Focus	Critical Essential Questions	Sample Supplementary Texts
				Ferdinand *Hidden Figures* *A Kid Like Jake* *Kinky Boots* *Little Women* (2019) *Love, Simon* *Moana* *Mona Lisa Smile* *Moonlight* *Mulan* *Queen of Katwe* *Wonder Woman* **Plays** Katie Cappiello, *Now That We're Men* Harvey Fierstein & Cyndi Lauper, *Kinky Boots* Susan Glaspell, *Trifles* Daniel Pearle, *A Kid Like Jake* Ntozake Shange, *For Colored Girls Who Have Considered Suicide / When the Rainbow Is Enuf* **Social Movement** #MeToo **Instagram** Carl Nassib announces he's gay
Ernest Hemingway, *Old Man and the Sea* Jack London, *The Call of the Wild* Herman Melville, *Moby-Dick* Henry David Thoreau, *Walden*	Amy Allgeyer, *Dig Too Deep* Yaba Badoe, *Wolf Light* Jamie Bastedo, *Sila's Revenge* Varda Burstyn, *Water Inc.* Octavia E. Butler, *Parable of the Sower* (Earthseed #1) Olivia Chadha, *Balance of Fragile Things* Georgia Clark, *Parched* S. D. Crockett, *After the Snow* Sarah Crossan, *Breathe* (Breathe Duology) Claire Datnow, *Red Flag Warning: An Eco Adventure*	**Nature and Environment**	What is the relationship between humans, nature, and the environment? What is the relationship between nature, the environment, and power? Should we act to protect nature and the environment? And if so, how?	**Short Stories** Isabel Allende, "And of Clay Are We Created" Terry Bisson, "The Toxic Donut" Ray Bradbury, "There Will Come Soft Rains" Adrienne Maree Brown, "The River" Kate Chopin, "The Night Came Slowly" Ernest Hemingway, "Big Two- Hearted River" Sarah Orne Jewett, "A White Heron" Jack London, "To Build a Fire" Saki, "The Music on the Hill"

Canonical Texts	Contemporary Texts	Unit Focus	Critical Essential Questions	Sample Supplementary Texts
	Carol Fiore, *Countdown* (The Skye Van Bloem Triology #1) Jordana Frankel, *The Ward* David Gilman, *Blood Sun* Diane Haynes, *Flight or Fight* (Jane Ray's Wildlife Rescue Series) Joan He, *The Ones We're Meant to Find* P. J. Hoover, *Solstice* John Kixmiller, *Protectors of the Wood #1: Phoebe Comes Home* David Klass, *Firestorm* (The Caretaker Trilogy) Saci Lloyd, *The Carbon Diaries* series Maja Lunde, *The History of Bees* Danita Maslan, *Rogue Harvest* Mindy McGinnis, *Not a Drop to Drink* Mike Mullin, *Ashfall* (Ashfall Trilogy) Mark Nowak, *Coal Mountain Elementary* Richard Powers, *The Overstory* Neal Shusterman & Jarrod Shusterman, *Dry* Tamar Sloan & Heidi Catherine, *Rising: After the Thaw* (The Thaw Chronicles Book 1) Camerona Stracher, *The Water Wars* Todd Strasser, *The Beast of Cretacea* Ned Tillman, *The Big Melt* Suzanne Weyn, *Empty*			**Informational Texts** Robin Broad & John Cavanagh, *The Water Defenders: How Ordinary People Saved a Country from Corporate Greed* Lucy Diavolo (ed.), *No Planet B: A Teen Vogue Guide to the Climate Crisis* Ralph Emerson, "Nature" Catherine Coleman Flowers, *Waste: One Woman's Fight against America's Dirty Secret* Dina Gilio-Whitaker, *As Long as Grass Grows: The Indigenous Fight for Environmental Justice, from Colonization to Standing Rock* Denis Hayes & Gail Boyer Hayes, *Cowed: The Hidden Impact of 93 Million Cows on America's Health, Economy, Politics, Culture, and Environment* Robin Wall Kimmerer, *Braiding Sweetgrass: Indigenous Wisdom: Scientific Knowledge, and the Teachings of Plants* Naomi Klein with Rebecca Stefoff, *How to Change Everything: The Young Human's Guide to Protecting the Planet and Each Other* George Marshall, *Don't Even Think about It: Why Our Brains Are Wired to Ignore Climate Change* Xiuhtezcatl Martinez, *Imaginary Borders* Sy Montgomery, *The Soul of an Octopus: A Surprising Exploration into the Wonder of Consciousness* Anuradha Rao, *One Earth: People of Color Protecting Our Planet*

Canonical Texts	Contemporary Texts	Unit Focus	Critical Essential Questions	Sample Supplementary Texts
				The Red Nation, *The Red Deal: Indigenous Action to Save Our Earth* Julia Rosen, "The Science of Climate Change Explained: Facts, Evidence and Proof" Michael Shellenberger, "Why Apocalyptic Claims about Climate Change Are Wrong" Vandana Shiva, *Stolen Harvest: The Hijacking of the Global Food Supply* Vandana Shiva, *The Vandana Shiva Reader* David Suzuki, *The David Suzuki Reader: A Lifetime of Ideas from a Leading Activist and Thinker* **Picture Books** Molly Bang & Penny Chisholm, *Buried Sunlight: How Fossil Fuels Have Changed the Earth* Lynne Cherry, *The Great Kapok Tree: A Tale of the Amazon Rainforest* John Coy & Natalie Capannelli, *If We Were Gone: Imagining the World without People* Cecelia LaPointe, *Ajijaak Crane* Carole Lindstrom & Michaela Goade, *We Are Water Protectors* Michelle Lord & Julia Blattman, *The Mess That We Made* Mélina Mangal & Ken Daley, *Jayden's Impossible Garden* Linda Elovitz Marshall & Elisa Chavarri, *Rainbow Weaver/Tejedora del Arcoiris* Jacqueline Briggs Martin & Claudia McGehee, *Creekfinding: A True Story*

Canonical Texts	Contemporary Texts	Unit Focus	Critical Essential Questions	Sample Supplementary Texts
				Baptiste Paul, Miranda Paul & Elizabeth Zunon, *I Am Farmer: Growing an Environmental Movement in Cameroon* Miranda Paul & Elizabeth Zunon, *One Plastic Bag: Isatou Ceesay and the Recycling Women of the Gambia* Franck Prévot & Aurélia Fronty, *Wangari Maathai: The Woman Who Planted Millions of Trees* Jan Reynolds, *The Lion Queens of India* Dr. Seuss, *The Lorax* **Poetry** A. R. Ammons, "World" Carl Dennis, "The Greenhouse Effect" Ralph Waldo Emerson, "Water" Robert Frost, "Nothing Gold Can Stay" Tiffany Higgins, "Dance, Dance, While the Hive Collapses" Denise Levertov, "In California: Morning, Evening, Late January" W. S. Merwin, "For a Coming Extinction" Gregory Orr, "The Pond" Robert Pack, "Eagle" Elise Paschen, "The Tree Agreement" Craig Santos Perez, "From 'Understory'" Dave Smith, "The Purpose of the Chesapeake & Ohio Canal" William E. Stafford, "In Response to a Question: 'What Does the Earth Say?'" Sylvia Stults, "Awareness about Our Environment"

Canonical Texts	Contemporary Texts	Unit Focus	Critical Essential Questions	Sample Supplementary Texts
				Sara Teasdale, "There Will Come Soft Rains" Melissa Tuckey (ed.), *Ghost Fishing: An Eco-Justice Poetry Anthology* Walt Whitman, "We Two, How Long We Were Fool'd" William Wordsworth, "Daffodils" William Wordsworth, "I Wandered Lonely as a Cloud" William Wordsworth, "Lines Composed a Few Miles above Tintern Abbey" William Wordsworth, "My Heart Leaps Up" W. B. Yeats, "Lake Isle of Innisfree" **Music** Louis Armstrong, "What a Wonderful World" Jackson Browne, "Before the Deluge" Johnny Cash, "Don't Go Near the Water" Crosby and Nash, "To the Last Whale" Miley Cyrus, "Wake Up America" Marvin Gaye, "Mercy Mercy Me (The Ecology)" Michael Jackson, "Earth Song" Bob Marley & The Wailers, "Sun Is Shining" Joni Mitchell, "Big Yellow Taxi" Randy Newman, "Burn On" Jon Prine, "Paradise" Cat Stevens, "Where Do the Children Play?" Three Dog Night, "Out in the Country" U2, "Indian Summer Sky" Dar Williams, "Go to the Woods"

Canonical Texts	Contemporary Texts	Unit Focus	Critical Essential Questions	Sample Supplementary Texts
				Art Christo and Jeanne-Claude, *Running Fence* Agnes Denes, *Wheatfield—A Confrontation* Robert Rauschenberg, *Earth Day* Lois Weinberger, *Das* über *die Pflanzen ist eins mit ihnen* **Dance/YouTube** Extinction Rebellion Protestors Dance **Film** *Avatar* *Chinatown* *The Day After Tomorrow* *Erin Brokovich* *FernGully: The Last Rainforest* *An Inconvenient Truth* *Planet Earth* *The Road* *Soylent Green* *WALL-E* *Whale Rider* **Play** Henrik Ibsen, *An Enemy of the People* George Sklar, *The Brown Pelican*

Appendix B

Sample Units with Supplemental Texts and Initial Questions to Prompt Democratic Discussion for Socratic Circles

Unit Focus	Supplemental (Informational) Texts	Initial Questions
Identities and Perspectives	CommonLit Staff, "Freud's Theory of the Id, Ego, and Superego" Rob Dekkers, "Influencers and Identity: Who Do You Want to Be?" Saul McLeod, "Classical Conditioning" Saul McLeod, "Self-Concept" Nausicaa Renner, "How Social Media Shapes Our Identity"	How are identities shaped? Is identity constant? What is the relationship between identities, perspectives, and power?
Voice and Agency	Tom Head, "Why Protest Events Are Not a Waste of Time" Moisés Naím, "Why Street Protests Don't Work"	When should we use our voice to act against injustice? What is the relationship between voice, agency, and power? How can we use our voice to act against injustice?
Combatting Anti-Black Racism	Nicki Lisa Cole, "Definition of Systemic Racism in Sociology" Devan Cole, "Graham Denies Systemic Racism Exists in US and Says 'America's Not a Racist Country'"	Is our society racist, and if so, how? What is the relationship between racism and power? How can we combat racism?
Freedom of Thought, Speech, and Expression	Britannica, "Permissible Restrictions on Expression" History.com, "Edward Snowden Discloses U.S. Government Operations" Adam Liptak, "Supreme Court Rules for Cheerleader Punished for Vulgar Snapchat Message" Richard Wolf, "What the First Amendment Protects—and What It Doesn't"	How are freedoms of thought, speech, language, and expression limited? Why might those in power limit freedoms of thought, speech, language, and expression? Should we act to protect freedoms of thought, speech, language, and expression? And if so, how?
Power and Corruption	John Antonakis, "Does Power Lead to Corruption?" Adam Grant, "Power Doesn't Corrupt. It Just Exposes Who Leaders Really Are" Christopher Shea, "Why Power Corrupts"	Does power lead to corruption?
Rebellion, Revolution, and Reform	Michael Brendan Dougherty, "Anger Is Justified, Riots Never Are" Alan Feuer, "How the Capitol Riot Suspects Are Challenging the Charges" Philip V. McHarris, "The George Floyd Protests Are a Rebellion against an Unjust System"	What is the relationship between rioting, rebellion, and reform? What are consequences of rioting? Can rioting be justified?
Persecution	Radley Balko, "There's Overwhelming Evidence That the Criminal Justice System Is Racist. Here's the Proof" Heather MacDonald, "The Myth of Systemic Police Racism"	Does our criminal justice system persecute some people more than others? In what ways can we act on behalf of those suffering from persecution?

American Dream	Gale Student Resources in Context, "How the American Dream Has Changed over Time" Kyle Korver, "Privileged" Steve Large, "UC Davis Economics Professor: There Is No American Dream" Mathew O'Brien, "The Great Gatsby Curve: Why It's So Hard for the Poor to Get Ahead" Robert J. Shiller, "The Transformation of the 'American Dream'" Al Tompkins, "What Is the American Dream in 2020 . . . If There Is One?" Mohamed Younis, "Most Americans See American Dream as Achievable"	What is the American Dream? How does a diverse America affect the stereotypical American Dream? Is the American Dream equally accessible? How can we help each other reach our American Dreams?
Genocide	All texts read throughout unit	Why and how does genocide occur? What actions can be taken to prevent genocide?
Physical and Mental Ableism	Edward C. Baig, "Video Games Are a 'Great Equalizer' for People with Disabilities" Jessica Chiu, "On YouTube, People with Disabilities Create Content to Show and Normalize Their Experiences" Agence France-Presse, "Myanmar Teen Soccer Star Defies the Odds" Perri Meldon, "Disability History: The Disability Rights Movement" Theresa Vargas, "This College Sophomore Wants to Change How We Talk about Disabilities"	What are kinds of physical and mental challenges? How are people with physical and mental challenges defying stereotypes about disability? What is the relationship between power and disability? What are ways we can advocate for people who have physical and mental challenges?
Gender Identity and Attraction	Belinda Luscombe, "Kids Believe Gender Stereotypes by Age 10, Global Study Finds" Michael Mascolo, "Time to Move beyond 'Gender Is Socially Constructed'" David M. Mayer, "How Men Get Penalized for Straying from Masculine Norms" Lindsey Tanner, "Not Just Boy and Girl; More Teens Identify as Transgender"	What are gender stereotypes? How are stereotypes about gender constructed and perpetuated? How are people challenging traditional/stereotypical notions of gender and attraction?
Nature and Environment	Julia Rosen, "The Science of Climate Change Explained: Facts, Evidence and Proof" Michael Shellenberger, "Why Apocalyptic Claims about Climate Change Are Wrong"	What is climate change? Do you believe in climate change? And if so, what should we do about it?

Appendix C

Culminating Writing Project: Beliefs and Values

For this unit, our focus has been on beliefs and values. We have explored the following questions: *What are beliefs and values? Where do we get them from? How do they shape our understanding of the world?* For this culminating writing project, you are going to write about some belief you have about society that you would like to implement or change, with an emphasis on social justice.

This has been a challenging year for all of us. We have been living through a pandemic, experiencing racial tensions in communities, and electing a new president. I know you have thoughts on these events, and now is the time to make your voice heard.

You are going to send an email or letter to some local or federal government official, school board member, or police department about an issue that challenges your beliefs and explain why you think there needs to be a change. If you were to write to a government official, you might want to challenge the idea of the electoral college and try to find a more democratic way to elect a new president. You might want to send an email to a school board member or superintendent about concerns around reopening schools due to COVID-19 and how to do so safely. What are some thoughts you might have on how to improve relations between police officers and civilians?

Your voice matters. The future is yours, and it is up to you to shape it. You shouldn't get to the end of your life and question whether you left the world better than the way you found it. These topics are tough for us to discuss, but they are necessary conversations to have.

There isn't an exact length requirement for this assignment. But keep in mind that you want to get the attention of the reader while also not throwing so much at them that they lose interest. I expect at a minimum: an introduction, three body paragraphs backing up your ideas with evidence, and a solid conclusion that makes your reader think after they have finished the letter or email.

Appendix D

Kayla's Social Justice Research Project

Project Overview

In this unit, you will complete a four-week research project focusing on a compelling question that falls under the umbrella of social justice. You will develop a compelling question after being introduced to several social justice topics and will complete preliminary research on the topic of your choice. You will embark on independent research, using guidelines set forth. You will compose a research paper that poses your question, presents your findings, discusses the implications of these findings for your question, and discusses action that can be taken related to your topic. You will present your findings at the end of the unit at a community research fair.

General Plan for Project-Based Inquiry

Pose Compelling Questions: At the start of the unit, you will spend two days on the process of posing a compelling question. On day 1, you will spend time familiarizing yourself with a social justice topic of your choosing. You will be given five general social justice topics to explore: child labor, access to clean water, voting rights, access to education, and poverty. You can select another topic of your choice; you just need to get approval from me. On the second day, you will be guided through the inquiry process, first brainstorming any and all questions that come to mind about the topic, and then refining and prioritizing questions until you have identified your top question.

Gather and Analyze Information: After identifying your compelling question, you will spend three days conducting research on your topic. As you conduct your research, you will complete both a source evaluation and a source analysis activity. The source evaluation process will help you determine first if you have selected a reliable source. The source analysis process will help you start to think about how you will use the source in the paper. It will guide you through picking out the most important information from the source and explaining how you will use this information in your paper.

Creatively Synthesize Information: After conducting research on your topic, you will begin the process of synthesizing information. This will take six days. You will start by first creating a detailed outline for your paper in which you will go through the process of categorizing your research and grouping it by subcategory. During this time, you will engage in mini-lessons that are aimed at fine-tuning certain aspects of your paper, such as thesis writing. Once your outline is complete, you will begin drafting the paper. This will take three of the six total days. During this time, you will continue to have mini-lessons on topics such as writing introductions and conclusions. By the end of the six days, you should have a complete draft (including in-text citations and a works cited page).

Critically Evaluate and Revise: You will spend two days evaluating and revising your work. You will start by completing a guided self-evaluation in which you will be given a set of objectives and asked to determine if your paper meets them. After a self-evaluation, you will conduct a peer evaluation, in which you apply the same standards to a work of a peer, while your work also receives feedback. You will also have a conference with the teacher to review important parts of your essay such as thesis statement, structure/organization, and explanation of evidence.

Share with the Public: You will finalize your papers using the feedback provided in the evaluation phase. In addition to finalized papers, you will create visuals and a presentation to share at our community research event.

Appendix E

The Corruption of Power: George Orwell's Animal Farm *and Samira Ahmed's* Internment *by Sarah, Anna Maria, and Bridges*

We decided to workshop George Orwell's *Animal Farm* alongside Samira Ahmed's *Internment* with the goal of creating an ongoing dialogue about the corruption of power. Our unit focuses on three essential questions: *What does the corruption of power look like historically and today? Why does power so often lead to corruption? How can we resist the corruption of power?* Through these critical essential questions, students will examine existing power structures in society—both in the United States and throughout the world. Students will also examine their own implicit biases and become active in dismantling corrupt power structures and preventing power structures from becoming corrupt. This authentic approach rooted in social justice repositions students from a passive position in the classroom to an active position in their community.

George Orwell's *Animal Farm* is a canonical text published in 1945 that is frequently taught in the secondary English classroom. This novella is an allegory that tells the story of a group of farm animals who rebel against their human farmer, reflecting the events leading up to the Russian Revolution and the Stalinist era of the Soviet Union. *Internment*, written in 2019 by Samira Ahmed and set in a near-future United States, follows a seventeen-year-old Muslim girl named Layla as she and her family are forced out of their home and into an internment camp.

Like *Animal Farm*, the novel highlights many instances of corrupt leaders and collective struggles among those who are made to feel powerless. For this unit focus, teachers can choose to read both *Animal Farm* and *Internment* or opt to just teach one or the other. We plan to teach both.

After introducing the unit focus on power and corruption with a read-aloud of Doreen Cronin's picture book *Click, Clack, Moo: Cows That Type,* we will begin a shared reading of *Animal Farm,* using an audiobook that is available through the county library on the Libby app. Students will have daily bellwork. Some days, students will be asked to complete a journal prompt that asks them to write a personal response related to the unit focus or to something read. Each Monday will be deemed "music Monday," when we listen and respond to a song from the unit text set. Each week we will also read one current news article related to a local or global misuse of power. Additionally, students will be exposed to one other genre each week, which may include a poem, artwork, or short story. The goal is for students to be exposed each week to at least four different genres related to the unit focus.

Students will be supported in reading both "with" and "against" core texts. At the beginning of the unit, students will practice reading "with" the text. We will model certain reading strategies such as inferring or visualizing. We will also teach a variety of craft and literary mini-lessons, drawing student attention to the use of simple sentences and allegory in *Animal Farm*. Having students read "with" the core texts will lay a necessary foundation so that they can then analyze the author's craft and consider perspectives shared. Students will also consider points of view in songs, informational texts, and other genres in relation to the core texts. Once students can consider whose perspective is portrayed and whose is missing, they will be better equipped to read "against" the texts and to introduce voices that are silenced. As evidence of reading "against" both *Animal Farm* and *Internment,* students will reimagine scenes from different perspectives and analyze how this changes the "narrative."

As for critical theory, we will view *Animal Farm* and *Internment* through feminist, historical, New Historicist, and Marxist lenses. We will teach mini-lessons on theoretical lenses, and student groups will view each text through a school of literary theory; we will then "jigsaw" groups so that students will see through multiple lenses. Students will apply their knowledge to create social ladders of the animals in the novel or to match certain female characters with common female stereotypes. Students will create visuals that represent their thinking and will learn from each group's findings.

Students will participate in a Socratic circle. They will use textual evidence from *Animal Farm* and *Internment* to discuss how the circumstances we are born into affect what we can achieve by looking at these circumstances as a system of power. Before participating in the circle, students will complete a privilege survey and read two informational articles that offer different perspectives on whether success and power are determined by hard work or by circumstance. Students will reflect on the Socratic dialogue and will be graded on their ability to respectfully disagree with their peers' differing opinions while listening to and considering different viewpoints. We will have students reflect on their responses to the privilege survey and consider reasons why they might believe something different from their peers and vice versa. We want students to begin to think critically about their own views and consider the circumstances that might have resulted in their thinking a certain way.

We will begin book clubs with a book pass during which students will rank *All American Boys* by Jason Reynolds and Brendan Kiely; *The Battle of Jericho* by Sharon M. Draper; *They Called Us Enemy* by George Takei, Justin Eisinger, Steven Scott, and Harmony Becker; and *Speak* by Laurie Halse Anderson. Though fairly different, each of these novels presents a form of corrupted power and will enrich students' understanding of the unit focus. Ideally, the diverse nature of these novels will allow all students to discover something they are excited to read. Once they rank the books, we will make the final decision for groups based on student and teacher input. Students will meet with their book clubs for thirty minutes each Friday after having twenty minutes for independent reading time in class. Students will be expected to complete the bulk of their book club reading outside of class, and they will also be expected to write two entries per week in an online reading blog. One entry will be a choice from a list of multigenre/multimodal writing possibilities that foster reader response and critical reader response, and the other will be a specific question that applies something we have learned in class—critical theory, reading with or against text, author's craft—to their book. These entries will serve as a basis for their group discussions.

During the last weeks of the unit, we will introduce the culminating research project centered on the idea of power and the corruption of power. This research project will consist of several parts, including observations, interviews, a culminating product, and a presentation, during which students share their findings with the class and an outside audience. Students may work independently or with a partner.

Students are to locate an example of power in their world—in their school or community. Research it; collect data; analyze and evaluate it. Is the power system or structure corrupt? Could it become corrupt? How? What can students do to either prevent or remedy this corruption? To conduct research, students will need to:

- Observe
  Think about someone in the community who is involved in the system of power identified. Using professional email etiquette, reach out to them and ask to shadow them for a day or evening.
- Interview
  After choosing your topic, identify people who either hold power or are affected by the system of power. Using prepared questions,

interview others. Listen to and learn from those who are experiencing these power relations firsthand.

- Research

  While conducting observations and interviews, you will engage in secondary research to help inform your final product and presentation. Create a reference list using either APA- or MLA-style citations.

Possibilities for the final product include an informational essay (5+ pages), podcast (~7– 10 minutes), or YouTube video (~7–10 minutes). If students have a different idea for the final product, they can discuss this with their teacher. Student research and writing will be guided and supported during writing workshop.

Last, students need to identify an audience beyond their classmates with whom to share their ideas. Think of people who have an ability to enact changes. Students will use the feedback received from their class presentation to prepare for making their voice heard beyond the classroom. Students will move from *talking* to becoming *participants* in social action. Students will receive the following materials to guide their social action project:

- Peer feedback sheets from class presentations
- Presentation planner
  - Brainstorm activity to predict what will come from sharing the presentation with an authentic audience
  - Graphic organizer for choosing the audience and finding contact information
  - Graphic organizer for drafting email and phone requests
- Mini-lesson on professional etiquette
- Reflection Assignment Sheet
- An outline for a final reflection on experiences

References

Anderson, J. (2005). *Mechanically inclined: Building grammar, usage, and style into writer's workshop*. Stenhouse.

Anderson, J. (2007). *Everyday editing: Inviting students to develop skill and craft in writer's workshop*. Stenhouse.

Anderson, J., & Dean, D. (2014). *Revision decisions: Talking through sentences and beyond.* Stenhouse.

Appleman, D. (2015). *Critical encounters in secondary English: Teaching literary theory to adolescents* (3rd ed.). Teachers College Press.

Atwell, N. (1998). *In the middle: New understandings about writing, reading, and learning* (2nd ed.). Heinemann.

Bagdikian, B. H. (2004). *The new media monopoly*. Beacon Press.

Barnes, D. (1992). *From communication to curriculum* (2nd ed.). Heinemann.

Bassett, K., Bigham, B., & Calvert, L. (Eds.). (2017, August). *Social justice book list*. The National Network of State Teachers of the Year (NNSTOY). https://www.nnstoy.org/social-justice-book-list-resources/

Beach, R. (1993). *A teacher's introduction to reader-response theories*. National Council of Teachers of English.

Bean, T. W., & Moni, K. (2003). Developing students' critical literacy: Exploring identity construction in young adult fiction. *Journal of Adolescent & Adult Literacy, 46*(8), 638–48.

Beers, K. (2003). *When kids can't read: What teachers can do*. Heinemann.

Beers, K., & Probst, R. E. (2013). *Notice & note: Strategies for close reading*. Heinemann.

Bellack, A. A., et al. (1966). *The language of the classroom*. Teachers College Press.

Bishop, R. S. (1990). Mirrors, windows, and sliding glass doors. *Perspectives, 6*(3), ix–xi.

Blau, S. D. (2003). *The literature workshop: Teaching texts and their readers*. Heinemann.

Bomer, R. (2017). What would it mean for English language arts to become more culturally responsive and sustaining? *Voices from the Middle, 24*(3), 11–15.

Bomer, R., & Bomer, K. (2001). *For a better world: Reading and writing for social action.* Heinemann.

Bonnycastle, S. (1996). *In search of authority: An introductory guide to literary theory* (2nd ed.). Broadview Press.

Borsheim-Black, C., Macaluso, M., & Petrone, R. (2014). Critical literature pedagogy: Teaching canonical literature for critical literacy. *Journal of Adolescent & Adult literacy, 58*(2), 123–33.

Boser, U. (2014, May 4). *Teacher diversity revisited.* Center for American Progress. Americanprogress.org/issues/race/reports/2014/05/04/88962/teacher-diversity-revisited/

Boyd, A. S. (2017). *Social justice literacies in the English classroom: Teaching practice in action.* Teacher's College Press.

Bruce, H. E. (2013). Subversive acts of revision: Writing and justice. *English Journal, 102*(6), 31–39.

Buehler, J. (2020). The critical work of YA literature. *Voices from the Middle, 27*(4), 19–23.

Burbules, N. C., & Rice, S. (1991). Dialogue across differences: Continuing the conversation. *Harvard Education Review, 61*(4): 393–416.

Cambourne, B. (1984). Language, learning, and literacy. In A. Butler & J. Turbill, *Towards a reading-writing classroom* (pp. 5–9). Heinemann.

Camera, L. (2019, January 18). A lesson in protest. *U.S. News & World Report.* https://www.usnews.com/news/education-news/articles/2019-01-18/teacher-of-the-year-organizes-protest-in-support-of-detained-immigrant-children

Cammarota, J., & Fine, M. (Eds.). (2008). *Revolutionizing education: Youth participatory action research in motion.* Routledge.

Carpenter, S. (2000). *Reading lessons: An introduction to theory.* Prentice-Hall.

Catte, E., Hilliard, E., & Salfia, J. (Eds.). (2018). *55 strong: Inside the West Virginia teachers' strike.* Belt Publishing.

Chapman, T. K., Hobbel, N., & Alvarado, N. V. (2011). A social justice approach as a base for teaching writing. *Journal of Adolescent & Adult Literacy, 54*(7), 539–41.

Christensen, L. (2009). *Teaching for joy and justice: Reimagining the language arts classroom.* Rethinking Schools.

Copeland, M. (2005). *Socratic circles: Fostering critical and creative thinking in middle and high school.* Stenhouse.

Dewey, J. (1916/1966). *Democracy and education: An introduction to the philosophy of education.* Free Press.

Duncan-Andrade, J. M. R., & Morrell, E. (2008). *The art of critical pedagogy: Possibilities for moving from theory to practice in urban schools.* Peter Lang.

Ebarvia, T., Germán, L., Parker, K., & Torres, J. (2018). *What is #DisruptTexts?* #DisruptTexts. https://disrupttexts.org/lets-get-to-work/

Ehst, E. S., & Caskey, L. (2018). Writing toward democracy: Scaffolding civic engagement with historically marginalized students. *English Journal, 107*(6), 38–42.

Eisenbach, B. B., Corrieri, C., Moniz, K., & Forrester, R. (2018). In search of identity: Connecting the classics to contemporary texts. *Voices from the Middle, 26*(2), 34–38.

Fredricks, L. (2012). The benefits and challenges of culturally responsive EFL critical literature circles. *Journal of Adolescent and Adult Literacy, 55*(6), 494–504.

Freire, P. (2001). *Pedagogy of freedom: Ethics, democracy, and civic courage* (Clarke, P., Trans). Rowman & Littlefield.

Freire, P. (2013). *Education for critical consciousness.* Bloomsbury Academic.

Freire, P. (2014). *Pedagogy of the oppressed* (Ramos, M. B., Trans.). Bloomsbury Academic.

Gallagher, K., & Kittle, P. (2018). *180 days: Two teachers and the quest to engage and empower adolescents.* Heinemann.

Gallas, K., Anton-Oldenburg, M., Ballenger, C., Beseler, C., Griffin, S., Pappenheimer, R., & Swaim, J. (1996). Talking the talk and walking the walk: Researching oral language in the classroom. *Language Arts, 73*(8), 608–17.

Gatta, C. D. (2019). Confronting bias and identifying facts: Teaching resistance through Shakespeare. In H. C. Eklund & W. B. Hyman (Eds.), *Teaching social justice through Shakespeare: Why renaissance literature matters now* (pp. 165–73). Edinburgh University Press.

Gay, G. (2010). *Culturally responsive teaching: Theory, research, and practice* (2nd ed.). Teachers College Press.

Gee, J. P. (1989). Literacy, discourse, and linguistics: Introduction. *Journal of Education, 171*(1), 5–17.

Gilbert, P. (1997). Discourses on gender and literacy: Changing stories. In S. Muspratt, A. Luke, & P. Freebody (Eds.), *Constructing critical literacies: Teaching and learning textual practice* (pp. 59–75). Hampton Press.

Gilles, C. (2010). Making the most of talk. *Voices from the Middle, 18*(2), 9–15.

Gilmore, N. (2015, September 17). Nielsen summit shows the data behind the children's book boom. *Publishers Weekly.* https://www.publishersweekly.com/pw/by-topic/childrens/childrens-industry-news/article/68083-nielsen-summit-shows-the-data-behind-the-children-s-book-boom.htm

Glasgow, J. N. (2001). Teaching social justice through young adult literature. *English Journal, 90*(6), 54–61.

Golden, J. (2008). A conversation with Linda Christensen on social justice education. *English Journal, 97*(6), 59–64.

Goodlad, J. I. (1984). *A place called school: Prospects for the future.* McGraw-Hill.

Goodlad, J. I., Mantle-Bromley, C., & Goodlad, S. J. (2004). *Education for everyone: Agenda for education in a democracy.* Jossey-Bass.

Graves, K. (2015). LGBTQ education research in historical context. In G. L. Wimberly (Ed.), *LGBTQ issues in education: Advancing a research agenda* (pp. 23–42). American Educational Research Association.

Greene, M. (1995). *Releasing the imagination: Essays on education, the arts, and social change.* Jossey-Bass.

Hynds, S., & Appleman, D. (1997). Walking our talk: Between response and responsibility in the literature classroom. *English Education, 29*(4), 272–94.

Ibsen, H. (2001). *A doll's house*. Project Gutenberg eBook. http://www.gutenberg.org/files/2542/2542-h/2542-h.htm

International Literacy Association. (2018). *Expanding the canon: How diverse literature can transform literacy learning*. https://www.literacyworldwide.org/docs/default-source/where-we-stand/ila-expanding-the-canon.pdf

Introduction to Literary Theory. (n.d.). Purdue Writing Lab. Retrieved October 14, 2021. https://owl.purdue.edu/owl/subject_specific_writing/writing_in_literature/literary_theory_and_schools_of_criticism/index.html

Janks, H. (2014). *Doing critical literacy: Texts and activities for students and teachers*. Routledge.

Kendi, I. X. (2019). *How to be an antiracist*. One World.

Knickerbocker, J. L., & Rycik, J. A. (2006). Reexamining literature study in the middle grades: A critical response framework. *American Secondary Education, 34*(3), 43–56.

Ladson-Billings, G. (1995). Toward a theory of culturally relevant pedagogy. *American Educational Research Journal, 32*(3), 465–91.

Ladson-Billings, G. (1998). Just what is critical race theory and what's it doing in a nice field like education? *International Journal of Qualitative Studies in Education, 11*(1), 7–24.

Lee, H. (1960). *To kill a mockingbird*. New York: Fawcett Popular Library.

Lewison, M., Flint, S. A., & van Sluys, K. (2002). Taking on critical literacy: The journey of newcomers and novices. *Language Arts, 79*(5), 382–92.

Lewison, M., Leland, C., & Harste, J. C. (2008). *Creating critical classrooms: K–8 reading and writing with an edge*. Lawrence Erlbaum Associates.

Love, B. L. (2020). *We want to do more than survive: Abolitionist teaching and the pursuit of educational freedom*. Beacon Press.

Macaluso, M. (2017). Teaching *To Kill a Mockingbird* today: Coming to terms with race, racism, and America's novel. *Journal of Adolescent & Adult Literacy, 61*(3), 279–87.

Macon, J. M., Bewell, D., & Vogt, ME. (1991). *Responses to literature: Grades k–8*. International Reading Association.

Macrorie, K. *The I-search paper*. Boynton/Cook, 1988.

Mantle-Bromley, C., & Foster, A. M. (2005). Educating for democracy: The vital role of the language arts teacher. *English Journal, 94*(5), 70–74.

Maples, J., & Groenke, S. (2009). Who is an American? Challenging middle school students' assumptions through critical literacy. *Voices from the Middle, 17*(2), 28–35.

Marciano, J. E., & Warren, C. A. (2019). Writing toward change across youth participatory action research projects. *Journal of Adolescent & Adult Literacy, 62*(5), 485–94.

McLaughlin, M., & De Voogd, G. (2004). Critical literacy as comprehension: Expanding reader response. *Journal of Adolescent & Adult Literacy, 48*(1), 52–62.

Mirra, N., Garcia, A., & Morrell, E. (2015). *Doing youth participatory action research: A methodological handbook for researchers, educators, and students*. Routledge.

Molden, K. (2007). Critical literacy, the right answer for the reading classroom: Strategies to move beyond comprehension for reading improvement. *Reading Improvement, 44*(1), 50– 56.

Morrell, E. (2005). Critical English education. *English Education, 37*(4), 312–21.

Morrell, E. (2008). *Critical literacy and urban youth: Pedagogies of access, dissent, and liberation*. Routledge.

Morrell, E. (2009). Critical research and the future of literacy education. *Journal of Adolescent & Adult Literacy, 53*(2), 96–104.

Moyers, B. (1992, March 22). Old news and the new civil war. *New York Times*, Editorial.

Mundorf, J., Beckett, B., Boehm, S., Flake, C., & Miller, C. (2019). From the voices of teachers: Envisioning social justice teacher leadership through portraits of practice. *International Journal of Teacher Leadership, 10*(2), 67–81.

Myers, K. L. (1988). Twenty (better) questions. *English Journal, 77*(1), 64–65.

Myers, W. D. (2014, March 15). Where are the people of color in children's books? *New York Times*. https://www.nytimes.com/2014/03/16/opinion/Sunday/where-are-the-people-of- color-in-childrens-books.html

Nachowitz, M., & Brumer, N. (2014). Teaching the talk, not the text. *Voices from the Middle, 22*(1), 15–21.

The New London Group. (1996). A pedagogy of multiliteracies: Designing social futures. *Harvard Educational Review, 66*(1), 60–93.

Nieto, S., & Bode, P. (2007). *Affirming diversity: The sociopolitical context of multicultural education* (5th ed.). Allyn & Bacon.

Noden, H. R. (1999). *Image grammar: Using grammatical structures to teach writing*. Heinemann.

Nystrand, M. (1997). *Opening dialogue: Understanding the dynamics of language and learning in the English classroom*. Teachers College Press.

Nystrand, M., Wu, L .L., Gamoran, A., Zeiser, S., & Long, D. A. (2003). Questions in time: Investigating the structure and dynamics of unfolding classroom discourse. *Discourse Processes, 35*(2), 135–98.

O'Donnell-Allen, C. (2006). *The book club companion: Fostering strategic readers in the secondary classroom*. Heinemann.

Older, D. J. (2013, December 3). Another world awaits: Towards an anti-oppressive SFF. *Apex Magazine*. https://apex-magazine.com/another-world-waits-towards-an-anti-oppressive- sff/

Owens, B. C. (2017, February 6). *Racebending and representation in comic books*. African American Intellectual History Society. https://www.aaihs.org/racebending-and-representation-in-comic-books/#:~:text=Racebending%20refers%20to%20the%20practice,with%20the%20practice20of%20whitewashing

Park, J. Y. (2012). A different kind of reading instruction: Using visualizing to bridge reading comprehension and critical literacy. *Journal of Adolescent & Adult Literacy, 55*(7), 629–40.

Pedraza, E., & Rodriguez, R. J. (2018). "We are not dirt": Freirean counternarratives and rhetorical literacies for student voice and schooling. *English Journal, 107*(6), 75–81.

Postman, N., & Weingartner, C. (1970). *The soft revolution: A student handbook for turning school around.* Delta Books.

Rhuday-Perkovich, O. (2017). Say that to my face: On teaching and learning diverse literature for empowerment and transformation (or, on feeling itchy). *Voices from the Middle, 24*(3), 25–28.

Robb, L. (2012). *The smart writing handbook.* Firsthand.

Rodesiler, L. (2018). Matters of life and death: Racism, patriotism, and policing in *All American Boys. Voices from the Middle, 26*(2), 20–24.

Romano, T. (2000). *Blending genre, altering style: Writing multigenre papers.* Boynton/Cook.

Rosenblatt, L. M. (1985). The transactional theory of the literary work: Implications for research. In C. R. Cooper (Ed.), *Researching response to literature and the teaching of literature: Points of departure* (pp. 33–53). Ablex.

Rosenblatt, L. M. (1994). *The reader, the text, the poem: The transactional theory of the literary work.* Southern Illinois University Press.

Rosenblatt, L. M. (1995). *Literature as exploration* (5th ed.). Modern Language Association.

Rycik, J. A., & Irvin, J. L. (2005). *Teaching reading in the middle grades: Understanding supporting literacy development.* Allyn & Bacon.

Schieble, M. (2010). Reading between the lines of reader response: Constructing "the other" through the aesthetic stance. *Changing English, 17*(4), 375–84.

Schmidt, L. (2009). Stirring up justice: Teaching students about interdependence through social action is a lesson that can stick. *Educational Leadership, 66*(8), 32–37.

Serafini, F. (2001). *The reading workshop: Creating space for readers.* Heinemann.

Shor, I. (1999). What is critical literacy? In I. Shor & C. Pari (Eds.), *Critical literacy in action: Writing words, changing worlds* (pp. 1–30). Boynton/Cook.

Simmons, A. M. (2012). Class on fire: Using the Hunger Games trilogy to encourage social action. *Journal of Adolescent & Adult Literacy, 56*(1), 22–34.

Simon, L. (2007). Expanding literacies: Teachers' inquiry research and multigenre texts. *English Education, 39*(2), 146–76.

Sinclair, M. N. (2018). Decolonizing ELA: Confronting privilege and oppression in textual spaces. *English Journal, 107*(6), 89–94.

Slack, D. B. (2001). Fusing social justice with multigenre writing. *English Journal, 90*(6), 62–65.

Smathers Library Gallery. (2018, October 22–December 18). *Black Educators: Florida's Secret Social Justice Advocates 1920–1960.* Gainesville, FL.

Smith, M. W., Wilhelm, J. D., & Fredricksen, J. E. (2012). *Oh, Yeah?! Putting argument to work both in school and out*. Heinemann.

Stachowiak, D. M. (2017). Social action and social justice: A path to critical consciousness for engagement. *Voices from the Middle, 24*(3), 29–31.

Stevens, R. (1912). *The question as a measure of efficiency in instruction: A critical study of classroom practice*. Teachers College.

Stone, N. (2017). *Dear Martin*. Crown.

Storm, S., & Rainey, E. C. (2018). Striving toward woke English teaching and learning. *English Journal, 107*(6), 95–101.

Styslinger, M. E., & Pollock, T. (2010). The chicken and the egg: Inviting response and talk through Socratic circles. *Voices from the Middle, 18*(2), 36–45.

Sumara, D. J. (2000). Researching complexity. *Journal of Literacy Research, 32*(2), 267–281.

Thomas, E. E. (2018). Critical engagement with middle grades reads: Who lives? Who thrives? Who tells your story? *Voices from the Middle, 26*(2), 13–16.

Thomas, E. E., & Stornaiuolo, A. (2016). Restorying the self: Bending toward textual justice. *Harvard Educational Review, 86*(3), 313–38.

Tierney, R. J., Readence, J. E., & Dishner, E. K. (1995). *Reading strategies and practices: A compendium* (4th Ed.). Allyn & Bacon.

Tovani, C. (2000). *I read it, but I don't get it: Comprehension strategies for adolescent readers*. Stenhouse.

Urrieta, L., Jr. (2009). *Working from within: Chicana and Chicano activist educators in whitestream schools*. University of Arizona Press.

Vopat, J. (2009). *Writing circles: Kids revolutionize workshop*. Heinemann.

Wilhelm, J. D. (1997). *"You gotta be the book": Teaching engaged and reflective reading with adolescents*. Teachers College Press.

Wilhelm, J. D. (2004). *Reading is seeing: Learning to visualize scenes, characters, ideas, and text worlds to improve comprehension and reflective reading*. Scholastic.

Wilhelm, J. D., Smith, M. W., & Fredricksen, J. E. (2012). *Get it done! Writing and analyzing informational texts to make things happen*. Heinemann.

Williams, T. T. (2004). *The open space of democracy*. Orion Society.

Wolk, S. (2009). Reading for a better world: Teaching for social responsibility with young adult literature. *Journal of Adolescent & Adult Literacy, 52*(8), 664–73.

Wood, K. D. (1984). Probable passages: A writing strategy. *The Reading Teacher, 37*(6), 496–99.

Worlds, M., & Miller, H. C. (2019). Miles Morales: *Spider-Man* and reimagining the canon for racial justice. *English Journal, 108*(4), 43–50.

Index

The letter *f* following a page locator denotes a figure.

Author

Mary E. Styslinger is a professor of English and literacy education at the University of South Carolina, where she directed the Midlands Writing Project and served as secondary program coordinator. She is a past president of the South Carolina Council of Teachers of English and currently coedits *South Carolina English Teacher*. Her research interests include interweaving literacy into the English curriculum, teaching English for democracy and justice, and serving marginalized and at-risk youth. She is the author of *Workshopping the Canon* and coeditor of *Literacy behind Bars*, as well as author or coauthor of articles published in *English Journal*, *Voices from the Middle*, *Language Arts*, *Journal of Adolescent & Adult Literacy*, *English Teaching: Practice & Critique*, and *Kappan*.

This book was typeset in AvenirNext, Myriad Pro, and Palatino
by Barbara Frazier.

The typefaces used on the cover include Trajan Pro, Freeland, and Pea Lopi.

The book was printed on 50 lb., white offset paper.